"Louis Roy tackles one of the more difficult questions of our time: How can one be fully human and profoundly Christian at the same time? Roy takes seriously both the psychologies of self-fulfillment and the movement toward self-transcendence. Anyone who desires to be both truly human and yet faithful to the Gospel will want to read this book and will benefit from its insights."
—DONALD J. GOERGEN
Aquinas Institute of Theology

"Louis Roy does a masterful job of debunking the common notion that self-transcendence and self-actualization are intrinsically opposed, and rather suggests that a proper understanding of each reveals their intrinsic and dynamic complementarity. In doing so, he explores a range of thinkers—from Aristotle and Aquinas to Lonergan and Kristeva—in an accessible way that yet honors their depth and subtlety. A rich resource for anyone entrusted with the care of souls, minds and hearts."
—JOSEPH J. GUIDO
Providence College

"In conversation with many voices from the disciplines of psychology and philosophy, Louis Roy demonstrates that love of self and love of other are complimentary, not opposed. He then engages the voice of Christian faith, asserting that believers experience this reality through the self-gift of a Trinitarian God whose very being is mutual giving and receiving of love."
—MARIELLE FRIGGE
Mount Marty University

"Are 'self-realization,' understood as psychological fulfillment, and a radical following of the gospel at odds? Can we be both enculturated and countercultural in a discerning way? For answers, *Self-Actualization and the Radical Gospel* a read. Louis Roy will provide the psychological and philosophical depth for an amazing synthesis!"

—CARLA MAE STREETER
Aquinas Institute of Theology

"An insightful update to a previous gem, Louis Roy presents an accessible roadmap toward authentic self-actualization within God's radical embrace. In helping the reader to understand the role of feelings, wants, and personal values, Roy leads us through the challenges of twenty-first-century living toward knowing ourselves and God authentically."

—SUSAN L. GRAY
Lonergan Research Centre, Ottawa

Self-Actualization
and the Radical Gospel

Self-Actualization
and the Radical Gospel

Second Edition

LOUIS ROY

▲ CASCADE *Books* • Eugene, Oregon

SELF-ACTUALIZATION AND THE RADICAL GOSPEL
Second Edition

Copyright © 2022 Louis Roy. All rights reserved. Except for brief quotations in critical publications or reviews, no part of this book may be reproduced in any manner without prior written permission from the publisher. Write: Permissions, Wipf and Stock Publishers, 199 W. 8th Ave., Suite 3, Eugene, OR 97401.

Cascade Books
An Imprint of Wipf and Stock Publishers
199 W. 8th Ave., Suite 3
Eugene, OR 97401

www.wipfandstock.com

PAPERBACK ISBN: 978-1-6667-3627-4
HARDCOVER ISBN: 978-1-6667-9439-7
EBOOK ISBN: 978-1-6667-9440-3

Cataloguing-in-Publication data:

Names: Roy, Louis, author.

Title: Self-actualization and the radical gospel : second edition / Louis Roy.

Description: Eugene, OR : Cascade Books, 2022 | Includes bibliographical references.

Identifiers: ISBN 978-1-6667-3627-4 (paperback) | ISBN 978-1-6667-9439-7 (hardcover) | ISBN 978-1-6667-9440-3 (ebook)

Subjects: LCSH: Self-esteem—Religious aspects—Christianity. | Self-actualization (Psychology)—Religious aspects—Christianity.

Classification: BV4598.2 .R69 2022 (paperback) | BV4598.2 .R69 (ebook)

VERSION NUMBER 091922

The Scripture quotations contained herein are from the New Revised Standard Version of the Bible, copyrighted 1989 by the Division of Christian Education of the National Council of the Churches of Christ in the United States of America, and are used by permission. All rights reserved.

Contents

Acknowledgments | vii
Introduction | ix

1 **Self-Transcendence Misunderstood** | 1
   Ill-Considered Devotion | 1
   Submission to Others | 6
   Disguised Self-Centeredness | 8
   Self-Annihilation before God | 10

2 **Self-Actualization Misunderstood** | 13
   The Need for Self-Actualization | 13
   The Search for Success | 14
   The Hunger for Immediate Experience | 17
   Moderate Egoism | 21
   The Influential Jean-Jacques Rousseau | 26
   A More Complete Diagnosis | 31

3 **The Tendency toward Self-Actualization** | 34
   A Consciousness Capable of Self-Transcendence | 34
   The Role of Pleasure | 36
   The Role of Effort | 39
   The Hierarchy of Values | 41
   Intentionality and the Psyche | 43
   Love of Self and Love of Neighbor | 45

4 The Radical Gospel: Historical Setting | 49
   Mission and Opposition | 50
   Invitation to the Marginal | 51
   Relationships within Communities | 54
   Suffering, Attitudes, and Behavior | 55

5 The Radical Gospel: An Interpretation | 57
   Motivation | 57
   Those to Whom the Message Is Addressed | 61
   Nonresistance and Forgiveness | 66

6 Toward a Synthesis | 73
   Love of Self | 74
   From the Ego to the Self | 79
   The Horizon of an Unsuspected Reality | 81
   Self-Gift | 83
   The Fascination for God | 86
   Happiness and Finitude | 88

7 Rhythms and Readjustments | 92
   Complementary Rhythms | 92
   Readjustments and Reorientations | 95
   The Role of Counseling or Therapy | 98
   The Psychic, the Social, and the Spiritual | 102

Conclusion | 106
Bibliography | 109

Acknowledgments

This is a new edition, with many revisions and additions, of a book that was published in 2002 by Liturgical Press and has been out of print for some time. It offers some clarifications as well as strong encouragement to those who take seriously the unique adventure that consists in maturing. In these pages, I will argue for a reconciliation between self-actualization and the radical Gospel, with a view to enhancing the reader's personal growth, while taking account of time, of successes and failures, and of various developmental factors. Although this book demands intellectual attentiveness and refers to respected thinkers, it presents a series of accessible, well-organized reflections on a topic that ought to be central to the lives of all Christians and of those among non-Christians who are seekers.

I am grateful to my fellow Dominican friars in Canada who, once more, have defrayed the costs of publication. Moreover, special thanks are due to Pierre LaViolette, who formatted and copyedited the footnotes and bibliography, and to Anne Louise Mahoney, who copyedited the body of the manuscript. Her unremitting attentiveness to detail and, mostly, her lovely friendship have graced many of my days.

Throughout this volume, unless otherwise indicated, italicization is by the authors cited. I follow the usual guidelines of inclusive language regarding people, either by employing the plural or by alternating "he" and "she." However, in accord with biblical language, God is referred to as "he." Biblical quotations are from

ACKNOWLEDGMENTS

The New Revised Standard Version, published as *The New Oxford Annotated Bible* (Oxford University Press), at times with slight modifications indicated in square brackets.

Introduction

In his tragedy *Antigone*, Sophocles has the Chorus declare, "Wonders are many, and none is more wonderful than man."[1] Indeed, human beings are worthy of respect and honor, in particular as they struggle in the midst of tensions between the urge for psychological balance and the call to become religiously radical.

The Gospel is radical in what it requires of believers. Its intransigence explains the attraction, the fascination, it has always exerted on those who seek an absolute. In fact, such people discover that despite enriching experiences and activities, life remains empty unless it is centered on a great cause or, more precisely, on a God whose goal for humanity merits the total consecration of their energies.

Apart from the believers who have previously staked their whole existence on the Gospel and perhaps have not felt let down by God, there are many who have been disappointed by social institutions or by the churches but who nevertheless are drawn to the Gospel. These people wonder if Jesus and Christianity might still have something to say to them. Yet they are often repelled by the radical Gospel, with its seemingly harsh and inhumane pronouncements.

There is then a tension between two views of ethics. On the one hand, psychological humanism is based on self-affirmation, acceptance of one's limitations, moderation, and the search for quality of life in the midst of globalization. On the other hand, the

1. Sophocles, *Antigone*, 124.

INTRODUCTION

radicalism of the Gospel emphasizes passion (in the two senses of this word): self-transcendence toward the Infinite, and generosity toward God and others. These two tendencies are neither incompatible nor easily reconcilable. Although the tension between them is an uneasy one, it can be healthy if it leads to inquiry and reflection. We can gain much from engaging this tension in order to both understand and accept it. This book will help its readers to grasp what a psychologically informed Christian ethics can be, both intellectually and practically.

These two approaches will be explored in these pages. The first, typical of contemporary Western culture, is the drive toward self-fulfillment impelled by psychology. (In this book, "self-fulfillment," "self-actualization," and "self-realization" will be treated as synonyms.) This ideal of self-fulfillment is ambiguous in relation to Christianity; that is, it can be either open or closed to the Gospel. The second approach, found in the very heart of the Christian faith, is the radicalism of the Gospel. This ideal has also proved rather ambiguous with regard to the development of the person. Therefore, we will attempt to interpret it correctly in its original setting as well as in its theological significance.

The subject matter of this book is not so much an ideal as a reality that is dynamic. That is why we shall proceed dialectically. In the first two chapters, we shall attend to the psychological tension between self-actualization and the radical Gospel, and we shall analyze inadequate ways of appropriating each of these two sources of inspiration. In chapters 3, 4, and 5, we shall probe an overall view that is at once biblical and philosophical. In chapter 6, we shall move toward a theological synthesis. While introducing permanent principles needed for a solution, this synthesis will prepare us for a return, in chapter 7, to the concrete problems that arise in putting a solution into practice.

Let us reiterate these steps more specifically. Since many people have been led astray in the implementation of ideals, the first two chapters present defective forms of self-transcendence and self-actualization, highlighting what can happen when these tendencies are incorrectly construed. Given that these chapters quite naturally carry a negative tone, some readers may want to begin with chapter 3 and the chapters that follow.

Chapter 3 describes what occurs when the tendency toward self-realization is functioning well, that is, when it amounts to a wholesome kind of self-transcendence, which favors an enriching exchange with the surrounding reality. Chapter 4 underlines the intransigence of the Gospel regarding the acceptance of painful situations and the renunciation of all that one possesses—and indeed of all that one is; it introduces the uncompromising demands of the New Testament and places them in their historical contexts. Chapter 5 explains how this radicalism draws its meaning from the reality of the kingdom of God and discusses certain forms that it takes in today's world.

Chapter 6 builds on the philosophy outlined in chapter 3 and on the biblical insights set forth in chapters 4 and 5. It delineates the relations that can be established between self-actualization and the radical Gospel. Opposed though these two outlooks may appear, nonetheless they can be synthesized by being located within the framework of a Christian view of life. Finally, chapter 7 deals with the practical aspects of bringing about self-actualization within a religious perspective.[2]

---

2. I also treat several of the topics in this book from a different perspective in Roy, *Embracing Desire*.

I

Self-Transcendence Misunderstood

The ideal of self-transcendence expresses what is most noble in human nature. Regrettably, in practice it is often characterized by defective forms, which can have serious consequences. This chapter deals with wrong ways of practicing self-effacement and self-sacrifice, which are passed off as self-transcendence.[1] It identifies typical cases of a self-transcendence that is poorly understood and badly lived out and gives a brief psychological profile for each case. I will call this distortion of our concern for others "altruism."[2]

Ill-Considered Devotion

In *The Four Loves*, C. S. Lewis presents the case of a woman whom he calls Mrs. Fidget.[3] He describes with black humor how the ill-

---

1. On self-transcendence, see Lonergan, *Method*, 99–101.
2. In chapter 2, we shall come across a so-called altruistic egotism, which reduces our concern for others to a minimum. Additionally, as will be explained in chapter 3, both altruism and egotism are incompatible with authentic love of self and with authentic love of neighbor.
3. Lewis, *Four Loves*, 73–83.

considered dedication of this mother caused her family to be tense and unhappy. After her death, the entire family, including the dog, began to relax. Was Mrs. Fidget simply the victim of her unenlightened zeal? In reality, her devotion was not totally selfless; it was manipulative and self-serving by projecting her interests onto the members of her family. First, she could look at herself with pride and entertain the idea of being the best of mothers. Second, her overwhelming generosity and her judgmental assertiveness won admiration for her, forced her children to please her unconditionally, and prevented them from criticizing her. She instilled in them a fear of disappointing her, a faultless person who was always right. Thus, they learned to practice a sad and inauthentic sort of virtue, based on intolerance of weaknesses, whether their own or those of others.

Psychoanalyst Erich Fromm discusses a similar case in *The Art of Loving*.[4] He considers this kind of "disinterestedness" a neurotic phenomenon. Far from being a form of love, it betrays an incapacity to love others, to appreciate their presence, and to receive what they have to offer. This attitude is accompanied by symptoms such as depression, fatigue, lack of motivation in work, and failure in matters of love relationships. Instead of attributing these symptoms to a defective way of loving, someone like Mrs. Fidget clings to her "disinterestedness," consoles herself with her immense efforts to give ceaselessly, and considers this disposition a character trait that can redeem her, in the midst of all her problems.[5] According to Fromm, such a person is paralyzed in her capacity for love and enjoyment, maintaining a blind hostility toward life and revealing herself to be self-centered, despite appearances to the contrary.

Fromm also notes the impoverishment that accompanies some people's experience of giving. Instead of envisaging a gift as a

---

4. Fromm, *Art of Loving*, 19.

5. About "the supposed motives," Nietzsche wrote: "Important as it may be to know the motives from which humanity has acted so far, it might be even more essential to know the *belief* people had in this or that motive, i.e. what humanity has imagined and told itself to be the real lever of its conduct so far." See Nietzche, *The Gay Science*, book one, §44 (his italics).

source of joy and an invitation to sharing, these people think that giving means "giving up" something—depriving themselves of it and renouncing it.

> They feel that just because it is painful to give, one *should* give; the virtue of giving to them lies in the very act of acceptance of the sacrifice. For them, the norm that it is better to give than to receive means that it is better to suffer deprivation than to experience joy.[6]

There is an unwholesome pleasure, an exaltation, almost a thrill in this form of giving, of thinking constantly of others, of feeling that one is needed. This thrill is often accompanied by workaholism, whereby hyperactive folks think they have no option but to respond positively to all demands made by other humans. How heavily the recipients are burdened by this excessive generosity, this tense presence, and the very gifts that are given! The giver does not let the receivers be autonomous, nor does the giver provide the freedom the receivers need to exist independently of the protective and monopolizing attention of the one who supposedly loves them.

Thus, Mrs. Fidget endeavored to control everyone in her family. At the end of the nineteenth century, Nietzsche denounced the self-control, imposed by someone else and then by oneself, that excludes freedom:

> Those moralists who command man first and above all to gain control of himself thereby afflict him with a peculiar disease, namely a constant irritability at all natural stirrings and inclinations and as it were a kind of itch. Whatever may henceforth push, pull, beckon, impel him from within or without will always strike this irritable one as endangering his self-control: no longer may he entrust himself to any instinct or free wing-beat; instead he stands there rigidly with a defensive posture, armed against himself, with sharp and suspicious eyes,

---

6. Fromm, *Art of Loving*, 19.

the eternal guardian of his fortress, since he has turned himself into a fortress.[7]

Nietzsche also diagnosed a superficial compassion that is not based on a real apprehension of the other person's situation. Again, what he says deserves to be quoted at length:

> Our 'benefactors' diminish our worth and our will more than our enemies do. In most cases of beneficence towards those in distress there is something offensive in the intellectual frivolity with which the one who feels compassion plays the role of fate: he knows nothing of the whole inner sequence and interconnection that spells misfortune to *me* or for *you*! The entire economy of my soul and the balance effected by 'misfortune,' the breaking open of new springs and needs, the healing of old wounds, the shedding of entire periods of the past—all such things that can be involved in misfortune do not concern the dear compassionate one: they want to *help* and have no thought that there is a personal necessity of misfortune; that terrors, deprivations, impoverishments, midnights, adventures, risks, and blunders are as necessary for me and you as their opposites.[8]

French philosopher Jean-Luc Marion offers us a short phenomenology of the gift. He comments on the giver and the givee (the one who receives) as follows:

> If he gives and is acknowledged as the giver, he at least receives the givee's recognition, even if his gift is never rendered to him; and, even in the absence of any recognition from the givee, the giver still receives the esteem of those who witness his gift. If by chance he gives without anybody acknowledging him as the giver, . . . the giver will still receive esteem from himself (for having been generous and having given freely). This esteem, which is in fact perfectly well deserved, will provide the giver with a sense of self-satisfaction.[9]

---

7. Nietzche, *The Gay Science*, book four, §305.
8. Nietzche, *The Gay Science*, book four, §338 (his italics).
9. Marion, "Reason," 101–34, at 103.

As a Christian, I cannot but remind myself of Jesus' advice:

> Beware of practicing your piety before others in order to be seen by them; for then you have no reward from your Father in heaven.... But when you give alms, do not let your left hand know what your right hand is doing, so that your alms may be done in secret; and your Father who sees in secret will reward you. (Matt 6:1, 3–4)

Many psychologists have reported that marriages fail when one partner tries to give everything to the other, to satisfy all of the other's needs, without asking anything in return. A person may sincerely believe that she is living out a great love as she tries to ignore the extent to which her own expectations are going unmet. She may come to accuse her husband of ingratitude or blame herself for the strain in their relationship. She may become vaguely aware that in systematically putting her husband ahead of herself, she is nourishing her partner's egotism. But she does not see clearly the conclusion that must be drawn, namely that this altruism is not the right way to express love.

Another common error lies in not taking account of one's feelings or in distrusting them. A person may tell himself that love is fundamentally a question of will, that it cannot be based on what he finds pleasant, on what he desires. It is true that we cannot rely on passing emotions. But we should not forget that there are also enduring feelings, which are fundamental dispositions based on value judgments, that, in turn, are rarely subject to change.[10] When positive sentiments of a transitory nature are lacking and one wants to maintain a conjugal relationship or a bond of friendship, it is important to consider the more profound inclinations and permanent value judgments that give orientation to one's life. If an individual fails to recognize and validate those dispositions, he may too quickly appeal to the force of will, thus falling into voluntarism. This fear of self-knowledge leads to self-deception and often accounts for an individual's rejection of any

---

10. See Lonergan, *Method*, 31–41.

sort of therapy, even though therapy would enable him to be a lesser burden to others.[11]

Submission to Others

Unconditional submission to the will of someone else is another harmful way of dealing with our intimates. George Eliot once declared, "Among the various excesses to which human nature is subject, moralists have never numbered that of being too fond of the people who openly revile us."[12] She also observed, "A proud woman who has learned to submit, carries all her pride to the reinforcement of her submission, and looks down with severe superiority on all feminine assumption as 'unbecoming.'"[13] This attitude invites someone to assume a position of superiority, from which it is easy to abuse others. As Gene Outka observes, the golden rule that says, "Do unto others as you would have them do unto you" is inverted to "Do unto others as *they* would have you do unto them."[14]

This is again a matter of false love, an excessive deference to the desires of others, coupled with a lack of self-respect. Fearing conflict or pursuing some tacit advantage, one is unwilling to express displeasure or disagreement. The opinion of the other becomes decisive since the need for approval and esteem is too great to risk criticism. And yet there is a reward: by deciding to render oneself useful without causing inconvenience or conflict, one hopes to win appreciation and to receive concessions and favors in return. In extreme cases, one totally escapes the anxiety of making personal decisions. In other cases, silent submissiveness generates, mostly later, sudden outbursts of rage and of accusation.

This negation of self goes hand in hand with the notion that it is intrinsically virtuous to put aside one's own needs, to overlook

11. On self-deception, see Roy, *Three Dynamisms*, 165–77.
12. Eliot, *Wise*, 108.
13. Eliot, *Wise*, 13.
14. Outka, *Agape*, 275.

the demands of one's emotions, to ignore one's inner thoughts. This renunciation makes some individuals feel admirable and thus maintains a false sense of self-regard. In reality, the self that one tries to value is weak and dependent. Instructively, Alfred Adler's psychoanalytic categories of inferiority complex and compensation allow us to understand that whenever we compare ourselves too keenly with someone who seems to be superior, we undergo a lack of self-esteem and of self-love. Compensation in terms of a fictitious self-transcendence is a dead end because it amounts to endeavoring to look good in the eyes of others instead of in our own eyes.

As a result, having failed to reach maturity, the person is unable to communicate adequately her vital drives, thoughts, and desires. Because someone is incapable of clarifying personal perspectives, he cannot really enter into the viewpoints of others, even while superficially accepting them.

In the life of a married couple, the rationalization of this weakness takes the form of disastrous principles. For example, thinking it will make the other happy, one gives over to one's partner all initiative and decision making. Thinking that loving means doing everything to please the other, one ignores one's personal tastes. Wanting only to be united with the beloved, one renounces an individual life with one's own interests, goals, and activities. The woman confines herself to the role of the submissive wife and absorbs herself in the tasks that flow from that role: cooking, housekeeping, care of the children, and so on. The man adopts the role of the breadwinner who has nothing to say about what goes on in the home. Such relationships often result in monotony, boredom, and dullness. The self that one would give to the partner becomes poor and unsubstantial. In this way, one loses not only oneself but also one's partner.

According to Wilhelm Reich, masochism consists in turning against oneself the frustrated aggressiveness that cannot be directed toward external objects.[15] Someone's aggressiveness has been repressed along with his sexuality, which is also an object

---

15. Reich, *Character Analysis*.

of fear. He is unable to channel the aggressive instincts. Hence, as pointed out before, at times he may explode with anger, belying his ordinarily submissive and gentle nature. In fact, what his relatives and neighbors witness in him is a deceptive gentleness based on a double hostility: hostility toward himself arising from the shame he feels for effacing himself, remaining silent, never criticizing, letting others make decisions and solve problems; and hostility toward those who profit from the submission he shows them.

Some people imagine that criticism of their ideas or behavior is a sign that they are not loved. They have little confidence in their own judgment. They are afraid of making mistakes, of being told (and therefore believing) that they are worth nothing. They exaggerate the importance of those who hold positions of authority. Hence, they cautiously follow the rules others make, never daring to think for themselves. They always obey the authorities, conform to the laws without reflection, and remain faithful to their obligations—without feeling free to reconsider them. Thus, they sink into passivity and routine. Initiative and change are excluded. The great advantage of this easy and secure stance is that they avoid being blamed by their own superego. Despite all these precautions, however, they cannot escape a more fundamental reproach, one that comes from their conscience: the awareness of having abdicated the better part of themselves.

Disguised Self-Centeredness

Despite appearances, the unhealthy modes of self-transcendence described thus far are forms of egotism. Although altruism seems to express devotion, it often covers up ways of protecting ourselves against the eventual disappointments or sorrows caused by unrequited love. Sigmund Freud clearly saw that when we desire someone, we make ourselves dangerously dependent upon the one we love. We run the risk of being rejected by that object of love or of losing it through unfaithfulness or death. Because of a deep fear of being hurt, we may have recourse to a radical solution: we make ourselves independent by displacing our highest value from being loved to loving.[16] By blocking up our natural attraction to other people, altruism dramatically reduces our expectations and precludes the possibility of bereavement, thus turning out to be a preemptive strategy.

Altruism can also be an attempt to affirm our own self by focusing on *our* peculiar ways of doing things for others, with the result that we shut out their reality: namely, what they actually are and need. The tactics pointed out above prevent communication and sharing. Defense mechanisms are set up to protect our areas of weakness and to confirm, in a bungling way, our personal worth. As Brené Brown points out, denying our vulnerability stems from a lack of self-worth, a fear of failure and of the shame that ensues, a nagging feeling that what we do or bid to do is never enough. Such feelings allow us to feel stronger than others and to despise those who look weak.[17] Like Mrs. Fidget, we are then not aware that endeavoring to solve other people's problems, instead of letting them try and perhaps fail, amounts to demeaning them. While sometimes seeming to be centered on others to the exclusion of self, in actuality we do not understand and love others as they are, with their weaknesses as well as their strengths.

The adoption of such disastrous attitudes can be explained historically by the pessimistic view of human nature found in many modern Western thinkers. Believing that the human being is fundamentally egotistic, these authors reflect in their writings a profound distrust of the self, sometimes to the point of self-contempt. Calvin contends that self-love engenders many vices, especially pride; he characterizes self-love and love for victory as "those most noxious pests."[18] Separating the supernatural from the natural, and exalting grace without taking account of its incarnate

---

16. See Freud, *Civilization*, 56–57.

17. Brown, *Daring Greatly*. The title of this book—not its subtitle—comes from a speech given by President Theodore Roosevelt in 1910. However, St. Eugene de Mazenod, founder of the Oblates of Mary Immaculate, had already proposed the beautiful motto "Leave nothing undared for the Gospel" in the nineteenth century.

18. Calvin, *Institutes*, book 3, chap. 7, §2 and 4.

aspects, they propose the artificial ideal of a pure and totally disinterested love that expects nothing in return.

This pessimism does not express Christianity at its best.[19] From the high Middle Ages, for instance, consider the writings on friendship by Cistercian monks and by the Aristotelian Thomas Aquinas: one finds a philosophy of love in which all-important aspects receive a balanced presentation. The pessimism of the late Middle Ages has left a deep mark on Western culture. The characteristic psychological outlook of North Americans is a reaction against this pessimism—an optimism that goes too far in the opposite direction. This point will be further discussed in the next two chapters.

Many people today have abandoned this tense striving for an ideal that contravenes so many fundamental aspirations. Nevertheless, this attitude continues to be a permanent temptation, and numerous new converts to churches and sects succumb to this inauthentic behavior. That is why it was necessary to delineate it and to show its defects. Is there a solution? George Eliot offers a clue: "When our indignation is borne in submissive silence, we are apt to feel twinges of doubt afterwards as to our own generosity, if not justice."[20] Some people are apt to wonder about their own open-handedness, fearing they are losing the essentials of their own selfhood.

Self-Annihilation before God

Before concluding this chapter, I will describe a *religious* form of the falsely understood self-transcendence.

Jacques Pohier uncovers the error of wanting to sacrifice everything to the Creator in the belief that God is the Absolute, apart from which nothing else exists.[21] This mindset is based on the idea of God as a totality, irrespective of God's work of creation.

---

19. For what I think is the Christian view, see Roy, *Embracing Desire*, 26–33.

20. Eliot, *Wise*, 58.

21. See Pohier, *God*, 65–67 and 291–95.

Pohier rejects this representation and offers an entirely different vision of God. Bestowing existence on what is not himself, God creates finite beings with a space to exist and to breathe. He does not choose to be so present to creation that he would wish that any expression of indignation on our part be borne in submissive silence. Having placed the human being among other human beings, God does not want to be "Everything" to the human person. Likewise, before Pohier, Simone Weil had written, "In a sense, God renounces being everything."[22]

Pohier notes that in mystical writings there sometimes occurs a transposition that is both subtle and unjustified. From the fact that creation is nothing without God, one deduces that creation is an illusion. Created realities are not illusions, however, unless one treats them as idols, expecting from them what one should expect from God. There is sometimes hidden pride in the determination to be indifferent to the attraction of created realities. In the last few centuries, Western monasticism often derailed as it negated human values. We find an example of that non-Christian attitude in Verdi's opera *La Forza del destino*, where Leonora, thinking she has lost her lover, Don Alvaro, for good, resolves to lead the life of an isolated hermit in a cave.

The mystics' dialectic of "all or nothing" can be experienced as a means of self-emptying in order to be exalted by the Father. The recompense that the person then expects corresponds to a desire bordering on megalomania. Moreover, having renounced the world and accepted being nothing, the disengaged person no longer risks losing anything. He poses as being detached from human beings in order to be attached to God; in reality, this detachment is a means of avoiding suffering. It reflects a mentality more stoical than evangelical, as C. S. Lewis notes in *The Four Loves*.[23] Such a person does not recognize the play of finiteness, of imperfect human relations marked by hopes, disappointments, confrontations, and negotiations—all of which cause suffering. He does not accept

---

22. Weil, *Gravity*, 79.

23. See Lewis, *Four Loves*, 167–71. He is nevertheless mistaken in attributing this stoicism to Augustine.

the combination of light and shadow that makes life in the world both insecure and demanding.

A similar ambiguity is found in the limitless command of the Gospel to "Be perfect . . . as your heavenly Father is perfect" (Matt 5:48). This sentence stirs up an acute sense of guilt in many Christians. Are they at fault because they are imperfect, limited, finite? Or are they guilty because they have consented to reprehensible impulses and actions? In the first case, we are dealing with a global and primitive sense of guilt, which does not involve actual sinning; in the second, it is a question of a definite, realistic, and adult admission of guilt.[24]

To accept our finitude entails that we recognize our need for other limited beings and realize that our desire for them is good in itself, although the consequences of original sin make it difficult to act on such desire correctly. Therefore, nostalgia for a life open to the infinite and entirely given to God is ambiguous. Contrary to what Pohier says, however, as sons and daughters of the Father, we can be divinized by the Holy Spirit without fleeing human finitude.

After all, that is precisely what Jesus experienced in his human life. He was the perfect Son accepting and living profoundly what is most simple, limited, and negative in the human condition. At the time of his temptation in the desert, he refused a messianic role that would have been prestigious and close to megalomania. But if this was a temptation for that sinless man, how much more believers must expect to encounter it in their lives! We shall return to this issue at the end of chapter 6, when we tackle the question of happiness and finitude.

---

24. See Roy, *Embracing Desire*, 74–77.

2

Self-Actualization Misunderstood

Although it is natural to seek to realize one's potential, it is important to recognize how difficult that is to do. For example, according to psychologist Abraham Maslow, less than 1 percent of the American people attain true self-actualization.[1] In striving for it, many misinterpret its true scope and are led astray.

This chapter analyzes the defective forms of self-actualization that result from a misdirected, though well-meaning and legitimate, human tendency. The main question here is: In a Western world whose culture is greatly shaped by psychology, how can we avoid engaging in the popular trip of self-discovery at the expense of a genuine interest in others and in God?

The Need for Self-Actualization

The well-known psychiatrist Viktor Frankl forcefully rejected the quest for self-actualization:

---

1. Maslow, *Psychology of Being*, 204.

> The main mistake of appointing self-realization as "the ultimate motive" is again that it devaluates the world and its objects to mere means to an end.... Self-actualization is an effect and cannot be the object of intention. Mirrored in this fact is the fundamental anthropological truth that self-transcendence is one of the basic features of human existence.[2]

In "its objects," Frankl includes principally human beings, who, according to Kant's categorical precept, ought never to become means because they are ends in themselves. So, concentrating on one's own self-actualization (alias self-realization) would inevitably devaluate other people. Frankl even makes bold to assert that "only insofar as a person is capable of ignoring and forgetting himself is he able to recognize anything in and of the world."[3]

Theologian Bernard Lonergan is more balanced when he states, "Genuine objectivity is the fruit of authentic subjectivity. It is to be attained only by attaining authentic subjectivity."[4] This surely amounts to a tall order. Thus, Jeremy Wilkins has this warning about Lonergan's statement: "His famous quip that objectivity is authentic subjectivity does not mean that we inevitably make the world after our own image and likeness, but rather that doing otherwise takes considerable effort."[5]

Consequently, we must say that whereas Lonergan and Wilkins envisage the necessary effort to develop a sound personal subjectivity, Frankl considers only the danger of a kind of subjectivism. It is therefore important to examine, in this chapter, modes of misunderstood self-actualization.

The Search for Success

In Western societies, self-realization is often modeled on a vision of life that generally brings about disastrous results. This philosophy

2. Frankl, *Psychotherapy*, 45–46.
3. Frankl, *Psychotherapy*, 50.
4. Lonergan, *Method*, 273.
5. Wilkins, *Before Truth*, 97.

extols success for its own sake and overlooks whatever ruse it takes to achieve it. Many people admire uncritically the individual who "makes it," despite the path followed. In the 1980s, Colonel Oliver North, who made a mockery of the laws of the United States in the Iran-Contra affair, was but one example of those heroes whose boldness aroused the admiration of the public.

The search for success is often manifested in efforts to acquire power and money. Such people find satisfaction in getting the better of others, in deceiving, manipulating, or intimidating them. They consider themselves more intelligent and stronger than others because they have this ability. Similarly, possessions can be symbols of personal worth. Houses, cars, clothing, the places one frequents, the people with whom one shares leisure time—all these advantages are enjoyed less for themselves than as signs that one is superior to others or belongs to an elite group. In short, the desire for power and possessions reflects the goal of attracting or even compelling the attention, the respect, and the admiration of others.

Let us also include in this category another type of person: the intense individual who finds self-enhancement through performance. Winston Churchill said that the adult who is in a hurry to excel was an unhappy child. This opinion is a little simplistic. More precisely, the adult who is in a hurry to excel was a child who was loved conditionally, that is, loved in the measure in which he behaved well, performed good acts, and met with success. As a result, such an individual draws more pleasure and pride from noticing his own good acts than from seeing what those acts give to others.

At this point, it may be helpful to distinguish egotism, which is a *psychological* deviation, and egoism, which is a *moral* deviation. The former naturally, but not inevitably, leads to the latter. The *egotist* is egocentric, me-focused, and narcissistic, yet does not necessarily intend to exploit others. The *egoist* is selfish, that is, self-interested to the detriment of others and devoted to his own advancement without regard for the well-being of others. Nietzsche defined egoism as follows: "Egoism is the *perspectival* law of feeling according to which what is closest appears large and heavy, while in the distance everything decreases in size and weight."[6] I think what he called "egoism" actually is egotism.

Gabriel Marcel stated:

> I must puncture the illusion, infinitely persistent it is true, that I am possessed of unquestionable privileges which make me the centre of my universe, while other people are either mere obstructions to be removed or circumvented, or else those echoing amplifiers, whose purpose is to foster my self-complacency. I propose to call this illusion moral egocentricity.[7]

In a perhaps unwitting allusion to Marcel, John Main also speaks of "the illusion":

> The great illusion that most of us are caught in is that we are the centre of the world and everything and everyone revolves around us. . . . This is a very easy illusion to fall into because in the opening consciousness of life it seems that we are understanding the external world from our own centre. And we seem to be monitoring the outside world from an interior control centre.[8]

Cyril Connolly wrote:

> To extract the greatest possible value from one's own life. This depends hardly at all on the nature of one's experience so much as on the quality of the instrument used to perceive it—the senses or the mind. One's own life will never be important while one thinks it more important than other people's. The egotist is self-corroded.[9]

Egotistic efforts to succeed often result in individual egoism and, on a larger scale, in the moral breakdown of society. We can draw up a long list of symptoms common to post-industrial societies: dishonesty and shady dealings in business and politics; unscrupulous ambition in the workplace; an exaggerated emphasis

6. Nietzche, *The Gay Science*, book three, §162 (italics his).
7. Marcel, *Homo Viator*, 19.
8. Main, *Moment*, 27 and 30.
9. Connolly, *Journal and Memoir*, 181.

on leisure activities and sports, along with a cultivated ignorance of socio-economic problems; efforts to achieve sexual prowess; abortion, abuses of contraception, and a low birth rate; and the breakup of marriages considered statistically inevitable. What do these symptoms reveal? Efforts toward self-realization that abort, despite appearances, because these efforts are detrimental to others and to the hierarchy of values. What one reaps ultimately is profound dissatisfaction, lack of self-respect, and the absence of peace and joy.

Instructively, Graeme Hunter distinguishes between self-respect and self-esteem:

> Self-respect is alien to the therapeutic mentality because it implies the existence of some objective scale by which moral conduct can be evaluated. You can't respect yourself without judging yourself by some standard. The therapist replaces self-respect by the subtly different ideal of *self-esteem*—the latter being a subjective condition of self-approval that can be generated and maintained in the absence of real merit or achievement.[10]

In the contemporary West, the ideal of self-realization is too often misdirected and is used as an excuse to promote the egoism of individuals, special groups, and social classes.[11] For some time, we have observed a new development: the group selfishness of elders without regard for the young generation, whose financial burden will be excessive when they begin to age, without health insurance or a social safety net, and perhaps in an irremediably polluted environment. This egoism is as destructive of the individuals who succumb to it as it is of those who are its victims.

The Hunger for Immediate Experience

The unbridled pursuit of varied experiences, with all their new sensations and strong emotions, is a crude way of seeking happiness.

---

10. Hunter, *Pascal the Philosopher*, 88.
11. See Lonergan, *Insight*, 244–63.

In a world where the daily routine can engender boredom and the feeling that the individual is merely a cog in a gigantic machine, numerous people take no pride in their work. Many have not learned or have not been able to find self-worth in projects planned and carried out in cooperation with others. To ease their boredom, the young and not-so-young lose themselves in whatever self-gratification lies immediately to hand. One might say that only the sensation of living intensely proves to them that they actually exist. Their esteem for themselves depends on their capacity to satisfy superficial desires. They even pride themselves on inventing new desires and finding original ways of satisfying them.

This form of self-realization is childish because it confines the agent to the present moment, excluding those pleasures and joys that require a certain amount of preparation. Certainly, every person must renew her imagination and emotions by plunging into the here and now to let her senses find pleasure in nature and to do enough physical exercise to become *healthily* tired and relaxed. But while this sort of break from the serious tasks of the day contributes to a well-balanced life, intemperate pursuit of sensation destroys this equilibrium. Feelings experienced in this way only provide the illusion that personal worth can be increased by striving for and obtaining what one desires.

Insofar as personal worth is concerned, in 2012, high school teacher David McCullough made a sensation in a commencement speech, during which he told the graduates, "You are not special. You are not exceptional."[12] His point was that the pursuit of self-worth is often deceptively justified by the ideology of exceptionalism and entitlement—an ideology that is widespread among adolescents and young adults. Instead, he proposed the practice of continually reading so as to find satisfaction and meaning in questioning, discussing, and, by so doing, engaging in mature thinking. His recommendation was relevant, although it merely reproduced Aristotle's secularist ideal of the good life and Rousseau's craving for living intensely, as we shall see further on.

---

12. McCullough, *Not Special*, 307. For his argument, see xi–xiii and 303–14.

Some engage in a search for profound meaning but, after a while, they end up in skepticism and give up the search. They are like Voltaire, who, for a long time, vainly tried to reconcile divine providence with the troublesome fact of evil; he arrived at the conclusion that the only thing we should do is, as his Dr. Pangloss recommends at the end of the novel *Candide*, the mere cultivation of our own garden (*il faut cultiver notre jardin*).

Frankl deplores the carelessness in fundamental education that has failed to teach many young people an appreciation of the healthy tensions that accompany any worthwhile human enterprise:

> Man needs tension, challenge. If he is spared tension in this society of abundance and air-conditioning which is ours—a society where man is cosseted and spoiled by the softness of modern civilization—then it is by other means that he will find that tension. The truth is that we of the older generation have wanted to spare young people the healthy tensions which arouse vitality and which they need; and that is why many young people have turned to unhealthy forms of tension.[13]

More recently, Bishop Robert Barron, talking with some irony about relativism, observed:

> Relativism leads to a kind of spiritual laziness. What gives a river its verve and energy is the firmness of its banks. Knock down the banks in the name of liberty, and the river opens up into a lazy, undefined lake. People might float on this lake, but they have no energy or sense of purpose. This is an apt metaphor for our society wherein toleration of each individual's program of self-invention is the supreme moral ideal. We put up with each other as we float on our separate air mattresses on the lazy lake, but we have no purpose that unites us in a common effort.[14]

The quest for immediate satisfaction makes one forget the importance of natural obstacles, which alone can give some tone

---

13. Frankl, *The Will*.
14. Barron, *Renewing Our Hope*, 260.

to daily life. Too many people are not ready to sacrifice time and energy toward an eventual result. No doubt they have not experienced what it means to anticipate, savor, and prepare for a long-term objective. The tragedy is that they miss the only means for escaping the deadly boredom that drives them toward immediate gratification. In the long run, superficial excitement will lead to boredom and disgust. And prolonging leisure time does not reduce those negative emotions.

Who could be completely duped by this hoax? How can one not become aware, on some level, of submitting to the conventions and roles imposed by advertising and by the dominant mentality? Many people want to ignore that this is a collective lie, as they have no hope that any other path will set them free. That is why they remain subject to an ideology of pleasure that seems to correspond well to experience. This anti-morality is a disguised morality; it inflicts guilt on people who feel they should have the audacity to satisfy all their desires. The right to happiness is expressed in the principle "I *must* have what I want." If one does not get one's slice of the pie, one feels foolish, ridiculous, weak, less sharp than others. According to the morality of pleasure, living consists fundamentally in taking and consuming, but, in the final analysis, paying dearly for the purchases. One can easily understand why advertising purposefully encourages it.

Craving instant gratification entails particularly disastrous consequences in the matter of sexuality. Many people do not, in fact, have the patience to accept the rhythms and stages that render human relationships deep and enduring. They are all the more incapable of understanding and respecting the final purpose of their sexuality, which consists in expressing and strengthening the mutual love and support of two persons as they raise a family and take up social commitments.

The thirst for pleasure makes people demand more of certain types of activity than they can provide. "Greed is an impetus and insatiable craving, exceeding what the subject needs and what the object is able and willing to give."[15] Not only does one become a

15. Klein, *Envy and Gratitude*, 7.

slave to a mass of artificial needs and encumbrances, but one tends ineluctably to abuse others. The compulsion to provide first and immediately for oneself destroys respect for what is most noble in others, namely the capacity to share deeply and to establish lasting bonds. Dr. Igor A. Caruso gives a psychological explanation of this process:

> The thirst for emotion in the neurotic is the result of the conflict between two vital attitudes. The first consists in wanting to re-live an unexperienced love; the second, in wanting to prolong the delight of being loved. This desire to re-live an experience is revealed in a particularly serious form in a person who has been unhappy or abandoned in childhood; it results in an insatiable thirst to be loved—one, however, that is profoundly hidden. This desire is especially acute in spoiled children and those who have been sacrificed to the egotistical love of their parents.[16]

As this quotation suggests, a person's insatiable need to experience emotion may be an effort to compensate for the fact that she has been insufficiently or badly loved. She is uncertain of herself, uncertain that she is acceptable and lovable. Fearing another disappointment, she avoids relationships where she might really be loved. Not believing in love, she contents herself with less, though perhaps seeking passionately this lesser object.

Moderate Egoism

In contrast to the people just described, we find the intriguing group of those who adopt a moderate type of egoism and who thereby cautiously pursue self-realization. Their education has endowed them with skills that permit them to enter harmoniously into relationships with others and to get interested in goals and undertakings requiring an investment of their time and energy. Think, for instance, of the brilliant creativity that is displayed in

---

16. Caruso, *Psychanalyse*, 75.

computer science as well as in the high-tech business. Nevertheless, such people often achieve self-realization at the expense of others.

In chapter 1, we illustrated an erroneous form of altruism as bringing about several distortions. We now have to contrast an erroneous form of self-realization with healthy altruism. Harvard sociologist Pitirim Sorokin observed: "No human group can survive without a minimum of altruistic conduct among its members."[17] He extolled "genuine altruism" and defined it as follows: "Genuine altruism is pure also in its motivation: altruistic actions are performed for their own sake, quite apart from any considerations of pleasure or utility."[18] He explained:

> When altruistic actions are performed freely, for their own sake, they constitute *genuine altruism*. When they are performed for the sake of pleasure or utility, – not because of the inherent value of altruism itself, – they are forms of *impure altruism*. In genuinely altruistic actions, of course, a certain amount of pleasure or utility may and usually does follow as a *by-product*. However, they are not the reason for the performance of the altruistic acts, as in impure altruism. Genuinely altruistic acts are performed even when some suffering or disadvantage is incurred by the doer.[19]

By contrast, moderate egoists generally function quite well. Most of them had a relatively happy childhood. They have not suffered much, and they are unprepared to suffer. Unless they are exceptionally ambitious, they do not take up major challenges; rather, they seize entertaining opportunities that will not involve too great a cost; to a certain extent, they are disengaged. They hold it as a self-evident principle that they have a right to happiness. Therefore, the misery of the needy does not keep them awake at

17. Sorokin, *Reconstruction*, 57.

18. Sorokin, *Reconstruction*, 59.

19. Sorokin, *Reconstruction*, 60. Such "genuinely altruistic acts" become impossible in a culture where the ideal for the human being is artificial intelligence, hence without sense of empathy, as Sherry Turkle, herself a retired professor of science of mind and technology at M.I.T., contends in Turkle, *Empathy Diaries*.

night. They pay no attention to inconvenient others such as Lazarus, the poor man who lay at the rich man's gate and merely desired to be fed with what fell from the latter's table (Luke 16:19–31).

A certain subjectivism affects this personality type. When these individuals carry out well the tasks they undertake, they are more interested in efficient functioning than in the objective good to which the tasks are directed. Many years ago, I heard a graduate student correctly observe that egoists, far from being inattentive to reality, are "cool schemers, shrewd calculators, and hard-headed self-seekers who, with detachment of intelligence invent and implement stratagems that work."[20] However, their primary objective is self-actualization, understood as self-reference, self-knowledge, self-confidence, self-inventing, harmony, spontaneity, creativity, personal growth, and full development of their potential. The principal criterion of their action is psychological, pre-ethical. To the extent that this criterion truly influences their motivation, they are unlikely to love well, because in their love for another they love themselves first and foremost. They think that it is more important to be happy than to perform good acts for those around them. Because they look out only for themselves or for the self-realization of their children as extensions of themselves, their egotism turns into a personal or family egoism.

Moderate egoists may follow this credo: "Be not egoistic, but simply egotistic, or self-interested, while being nice and not doing harm to others." But in reality, in cultivating their individual desires, they are likely to become blind to the harm they do to others. One cannot be at the same time egotistic and actively concerned for the good of others, least of all in a world where the poor tend to be segregated and kept out of sight. Prior to any moral consideration, these two attitudes—egotism and concern—are mutually exclusive on the psychological level. Even if one knows that individual interest, correctly understood, demands that one at least set limits to the misery of the poor, it remains true in any economic system that the excessive prosperity of some exists to the detriment of others.

20. Her name is Pauline Sullivan, but I have been unable to trace her.

Dr. Hans Selye, who has conducted experiments on stress at McGill University in Montreal, has tried to justify this morality of individual interest by talking about "altruistic egotism." He claims that the amalgamation of these two apparently contradictory principles provides guidance for one's behavior.

> Once he fully understands the philosophy of egotistic altruism, he is no longer ashamed of being an egotist. He admits to being self-centered and acts primarily for his own good; he greedily collects a fortune to assure his personal freedom and capacity for survival under the most satisfying conditions, but he does so through amassing an army of friends. No one will make personal enemies if his egotism, his compulsive hoarding of valuables, manifests itself only by inciting love, goodwill, gratitude, respect, and all other positive feelings that render him useful and often indispensable to his neighbors.[21]

Only a very small fraction of the world's population can put such principles into practice. Who, in fact, is capable of collecting "a fortune to assure his personal freedom"? And how can the masses who remain in poverty manage to live, according to Selye's view, "under the most satisfying conditions"? Far from being universal, as he proclaims it to be while invoking "the unassailable laws of Nature,"[22] such a moral system justifies the wealth of creditors and puts a weapon into the hands of those who are defending their privileges.

Psychologist Lee Kirkpatrick termed this basic attitude "reciprocal altruism" and denounced its dangers:

> The principal threat to reciprocal altruism, from an evolutionary perspective [Kirkpatrick's perspective], is the counterstrategy of *cheating*. This is what prevents pure, indiscriminate altruism from evolving in a way that would otherwise be "good for the group." An individual (and his or her genes) can be wildly successful by

---

21. Selye, *Stress*, 115–16.
22. Selye, *Stress*, 115.

enjoying a free ride, taking the benefits of others' do-gooding without incurring the costs.[23]

The philosophy, adopted by Selye and by many of our contemporaries, is a valid one: it was also the philosophy of the English philosopher Thomas Hobbes, who lived in the seventeenth century, and it was taken up again by Sigmund Freud.[24] Hobbes and Freud view the human person not as an essentially relational being but as an individualist whose primary instinct is to preserve his biological existence and satisfy his desires. In a world where particular goods are limited, individuals must coexist. This supposes that they respect rights, contracts, and rules. Normally, these individualists would be totally egoistic. However, to avoid making too many enemies and to survive in society, they temper their egoism with a modicum of altruism. I am using "egoism" because I find Selye's "egotistic altruism" indistinguishable from moderate egoism.

Selye, then, proposes a new version of that pessimistic philosophy. Unlike Hobbes, but like Locke,[25] however, he colors it with a moderate optimism. Locke's philosophy underlies the rationale for Anglo-Saxon democracies. It is essentially individualistic: it considers groups and societies to be associations of individuals who freely accept social contracts. In this framework, the continuity of human bonds always appears precarious; union and separation can rapidly succeed one another. People do not trust commitments of long duration; they easily justify the dissolving of relationships in marriage, family life, friendship, business, and politics. Their sympathy for others does not include any personal attachment, so they are capable of avoiding real compassion as well as the suffering (passion) that is intrinsic to it. They remain emotionally aloof.

As Christopher Lasch points out, "freedom of choice" means "keeping your options open."[26] Readers of Saint-Exupéry's *The*

23. Kirkpatrick, *Attachment*, 252.
24. See Hobbes, *Leviathan*, and Freud, *Civilization*.
25. See Locke, *Second Treatise*, §11, 13, 15, 16, and 19.
26. Lasch, *The Minimal Self*, 38. For a fascinating documentation and discussion of such attitudes, see Bellah et al., *Habits of the Heart*.

Little Prince could say that the moral principle has become "I am *not* responsible for the rose I have tamed."[27] The idea of autonomy, which is not inherently bad, here retains the connotation of personal independence. Dependence and even interdependence are perceived as dangerous: to depend on others and on God is to expose oneself to frustration and deception. Thus, Illtyd Trethowan explains:

> Real self-preservation is the handing over of ourselves to God, which means the taking over of ourselves by God without interference on our part. It is this interference which is effected by the negative power, the power of refusal, but it represents itself to the sinner as the means to a positive advantage, the maintenance of his own independence. Moving out from oneself requires a kind of courage, and the sinner is not prepared to make the effort.[28]

The Influential Jean-Jacques Rousseau

A remarkable instance of moderate egoism, which is nobler than Selye's, is that of Jean-Jacques Rousseau, who nonetheless has the merit of having distinguished between *amour de soi* (self-love), which he recommends, and *amour-propre* (pride), which he warns against. He wrote:

> One must not confuse pride (*amour-propre*) and self-love (*amour de soi*), two passions very different in their nature and in their effects. Self-love is a natural sentiment which prompts every animal to watch over its own conservation and which, directed in man by reason and modified by pity, produces humanity and virtue. Pride is only a relative, artificial sentiment born in society, a sentiment which prompts each individual to attach more importance to himself than to anyone else.[29]

27. de Saint-Exupéry, *The Little Prince*, 71.
28. Trethowan, *Absolute Value*, 146.
29. Rousseau, *A Discourse on Inequality*, 167.

It is almost impossible to translate *amour-propre* into English; for Rousseau, it implies comparing oneself with others, wanting to feel superior—namely, entertaining vanity, being envious, and using power over them to demonstrate and buttress one's pseudo-preeminence. More than a thousand years before Rousseau, St. Augustine offered sound observations about the risk of comparing oneself with others:

> We could or can have the weakness of soul or body that we see in someone else. . . . There is no one who could not possess a good quality that you do not yet possess, even if it is concealed, which could make him unquestionably superior to you. This consideration is useful for breaking down and vanquishing pride, so that you do not think that, because in fact your good qualities stand out and are apparent, another person does not have any good qualities; they may be concealed and perhaps more impressive, causing him to rise above you, even though you do not know it.[30]

Rousseau justifiably stresses the primacy of love of self (*amour de soi*) and individual well-being in human motivation:

> When the strength of an expansive soul makes me identify myself with my fellow, and I feel that I am, so to speak, in him, it is in order not to suffer that I do not want him to suffer. I am interested in him for love of myself, and the reason for the precept is in nature itself, which inspires in me the desire of my well-being in whatever place I feel my existence.[31]

Feeling one's existence amounts to feeling fully alive, as does the "noble savage" or Rousseau himself, happily walking in a wood.[32]

This "love of myself" may be a reaction against Jansenist Christianity, namely against Blaise Pascal's unduly pessimistic account of natural love viewed as opposed to charity. This rejection of Calvinistic supernaturalism opened the way to Rousseau's

30. Augustine, *Responses*, question 70, §4 and 5.
31. Rousseau, *Emile*, book IV, 235, note.
32. See Rousseau, *Reveries*.

naturalistic praise of love of self as basically good so long as it does not degenerate into egocentric love, of which society is guilty. As a result, Pascal's excessive emphasis on human selfishness was followed, half a century later, by Rousseau's passionate defense of the goodness of human nature.

Rousseau endeavors to balance self-centeredness with compassion for others as he states: "The first of all cares is the care for oneself. Nevertheless, how many times does the inner voice [of our conscience] tell us that, in doing our good at another's expense, we do wrong!"[33] For him, this "care for oneself" derives from an arresting awareness of one's bodily existence, whose expressiveness brings about a sense of biological fulfillment. Elsewhere, he writes: "I can perceive [in the human soul] two principles antecedent to reason: the first gives us an ardent interest in our own wellbeing and our own preservation, the second inspires in us a natural aversion to seeing any other sentient being perish or suffer, especially if it is one of our kind."[34]

Logically, then, Rousseau praises "pity" (meaning "compassion") and observes, with respect to Jesus' Golden Rule (Matt 7:12):

> It is pity ["pitié" in French] which, in place of that noble maxim of rational justice, "Do to others as you would have them do unto you," inspires all men with this other maxim of natural goodness, much less perfect but perhaps more useful: "Do good to yourself with as little possible harm to others."[35]

This maxim applies to the current emphasis on benefiting from other people's attitudes that are nice, soothing, and reassuring and on abstaining from criticizing other people's behavior. Thus, Rousseau's Vicaire Savoyard—a kind and charming person—believes in the permanent goodness of human nature and in the unfailing sincerity of individual conscience.[36] Rousseau's self-

---

33. Rousseau, *Emile*, book IV, 286.
34. Rousseau, *A Discourse on Inequality*, 70.
35. Rousseau, *A Discourse on Inequality*, 101.
36. Rousseau, *Creed*.

centered attitude is the origin of the Western importance attached to "feeling good," which is an ambiguous desire. Rousseau himself remained self-centered as he abandoned his own children.

This self-centeredness is exemplified in what Eva Moskowitz dubs "worship of the psyche," "psychological idolatry," and "the therapeutic gospel" in a book that is an eye-opener but is nonetheless too negative with regard to the search for self-worth, which is good in itself and about which she says next to nothing. For all her negative attitude, she is indeed right when she notes: "The therapeutic gospel . . . robs us of the ability to make serious moral judgments." According to her diagnosis, only one thing is wrong in the quest for happiness: "The indulgence of any feeling that causes unhappiness to ourselves is always wrong. Outside of the therapeutic there is no good and evil. The therapeutic morality, of course, focuses our attention on the private life, blinding us to the larger, public good."[37] I will address this issue of blindness in the last section of chapter 7.

In a recent book, Tara Isabella Burton described today's "wellness culture" as particularly illustrated by "SoulCycle," which she rightly claimed is both a business and a movement with religious overtones. Her description of it clearly evokes what a twenty-first-century Rousseau would say:

> It's a theology, fundamentally, of division: the authentic, intuitional *self* – both body and soul – and the artificial, malevolent forces of *society, rules,* and *expectations.* We are born good, but we are tricked, by Big Pharma, by processed food, by civilization itself, into living something that falls short of our best life. Our sins, if they exist at all, lie in insufficient self-attention or self-care: false modesty, undeserved humilities, refusing to shine bright. We have not merely the inalienable right but the moral responsibility to take care of ourselves before directing any attention to others.[38]

---

37. Moskowitz, *Therapy*, 7; see also 283–84.
38. Burton, *Strange Rites*, 94.

Reducing human authenticity to a sincerity that is equated with emotional honesty is a recipe for disaster. Underlying moderate egoism, we find, in people less experienced than Rousseau, a simplistic kind of self-interest, which counsels, "Be egoistic; you yourself will be happy and others will only be the better for it! Think first and above all of your own personal interest." Still, the primacy of personal interest brings about the inexorable outcome, "You yourself will be dissatisfied and others will only fare worse!" This ruinous stance contrasts with the better rule of life, which might be phrased "Think both of others and of yourself inasmuch as a well-ordered self-love requires it."

Going beyond Rousseau's insights, Gabriel Marcel declared:

> Fundamentally, I have no reason to set any particular store by myself, except in so far as I know that I am loved by other beings who are loved by me. Love of self can have a true foundation only by using others as a medium, and that medium is our only safeguard against ego-centrism and our only assurance that it will have the character of lucidity which otherwise it inevitably loses.[39]

Or, as Rowan Williams, speaking of "a Christian enlightened self-interest," put it, "an unjust and unlawful system may bring profit in the short term, but it injures and destroys souls in the long term." Consequently and practically, Williams stated, "I stop taking it for granted that how I define what's good for me sets the agenda for everyone else, and I learn to see that there is no good for me that doesn't involve good for others."[40] Interestingly, Aristotle had already discovered and expressed that well-understood self-love means opting for the highest part of oneself, the part that is capable of actually loving other persons. We shall return to Aristotle in chapter 6.

---

39. Marcel, *Mystery*, 9. It was the Gifford Lecture given at the University of Aberdeen in 1950.

40. Williams, *Luminaries*, 83 and 18.

A More Complete Diagnosis

So far, we have explored various forms of self-actualization that end in at least partial failure. Very often, preference is given to lesser, materialistic goods, such as health, security, comfort, entertainment, sexual pleasure, and possessing others, thus reducing them to the status of objects. Blind to their more profound dimension, these individuals deprive themselves and others of the spiritual aspect of reality and thus lose appreciation of life's rich value. They look at reality through the wrong end of the telescope and consequently belittle the highest values.

What is fundamentally lacking in this outlook is attention to the objective aspects of self-transcendence. It is important to observe, however, that the reduction of the *objective* pole is accompanied by a caricature of the *subjective* pole.[41] The self that attempts to realize itself without respect for the objectivity of others does not respect its own subjectivity. Jean Piaget clearly states:

> Through an apparently paradoxical mechanism whose parallel we have described apropos of the egocentrism of thought of the older child, it is precisely when the subject is most self-centered that he knows himself the least, and it is to the extent that he discovers himself that he places himself in the universe and constructs it by virtue of that fact. In other words egocentrism signifies the absence of both self-perception and objectivity, whereas acquiring possession of the object as such is on a par with the acquisition of self-perception.[42]

What is developed is not the whole of one's personal potential but rather a truncated subject, inattentive to its own questions, both intellectual and moral, and little adjusted to the demands of the unconscious. This limitation is often rationalized by means of reference to needs. A person tells himself, "I need this success, this experience, this entertainment, this thing, this person." In

---

41. Recall what has been said about the objective and the subjective in the first section of this chapter.

42. Piaget, *Construction of Reality*, xii. My attention was drawn to this text by Conn, *Conscience*, 104.

deluding himself, he turns a deaf ear to the important appeals trying to make themselves heard from the depths of his being.

In a psychologizing culture, materialism isolates certain psychological principles, good in themselves, in order to justify itself anew; this is called "psychologism." The psychic functioning is separated from the moral sense. Certainly, psychologists are right to put aside matters of morality for a time during the course of therapy to let the actual motivation emerge. But once these motives are recognized—an important aspect of self-knowledge—morality should be addressed. One must resist the conclusion that human beings *have to* base their decisions on motives that are dominant in them. The motives themselves often need to be examined.

Such determinism is not to be found except in the case of a serious compulsion. Faced by differing motivations, which tend in various and even opposed directions, a normal person remains free regarding what action to take. Using the moral sense, which forms part of her intellectual equipment, she considers and compares the different actions she might choose. She then makes real choices, exercising true liberty in the face of the demands under examination. All human freedom is obviously conditioned by motives. Motives are not unchangeable, however; they can, in fact, be modified as one becomes dissatisfied with their consequences, inquires into their true nature, and traces them down to their origins. Such a change takes a long time and calls for much hope.

Psychologism is a bad use of psychology. Concentrating *only* on the psychological advantages to be drawn from experience, it serves to justify the manipulation of the sense of good and evil. This manipulation becomes easier the less one understands the profound responsibilities of the human being. Psychologism gains nothing from its one-sided view of reality. In fact, trying to separate psychological functioning from its ethical context creates problems even on the psychological level. It damages not only rationality but even the psychological functions that interact with it. Lack of attention to moral responsibility and accountability can only impede self-realization because concentrating solely on psychological satisfaction prevents feelings of deep moral satisfaction from playing their indispensable role.

Moreover, genuine moral responsibility, which allows for the overcoming of egoism, requires love of oneself. Concerning the presumably selfish individual, Erich Fromm asks, "Is his selfishness identical with self-love or is it not caused by the very lack of it?"[43] Whenever love for oneself is lacking, we can expect aberrations of both self-transcendence and self-actualization, in which the ego clumsily endeavors to assert itself through its accomplishments. Because it has been loved only conditionally, it craves recognition; it becomes self-assertive, with pride and arrogance. In its obsession to give or to take—released in awkward expressions of either generosity or egoism—it seeks continually to prove its own worth to itself and thus remains self-absorbed, narcissistic, and contracted upon itself. Perhaps we can compare this self-absorption to living in a windowless house.

In this chapter, I have endeavored to show that misconstrued self-actualization can degenerate into an unsatisfying pursuit of individual accomplishments, experiences, and pleasures, with the aim of consolidating one's defective self-esteem. Our provisionary diagnosis has broached a subject that will be more lengthily unpacked in our next chapter, as we analyze components of self-transcendence such as pleasure, effort, values, intentionality, and the psyche. In so doing, we shall be in a position to demonstrate the complementarity between love of self and love of neighbor.

---

43. Fromm, *Man for Himself*, 128.

3

The Tendency toward Self-Actualization

Notwithstanding the defective forms pointed out in the preceding chapters, the twofold concern for self-transcendence and self-actualization reveals the presence in the human being of a deep and positive dynamism. This chapter explores its strengths and implications.

A Consciousness Capable of Self-Transcendence

Despite the lack of conceptual precision that one finds occasionally in Abraham Maslow, this psychologist is a good guide for describing self-actualization. He remarks that it is gratifying to be drawn, interested, concentrated, and absorbed in a captivating experience. The experience might take the form of a film, a novel, a football game, or, more deeply, a sort of ecstasy—what Maslow calls a "peak experience." In his view, self-transcendence can occur whenever an activity causes you to forget yourself and go out of yourself to concentrate on a problem, an action, a subject, or a person. This transcendence in no way constitutes a diminishment or impoverishment; on the contrary, the more the self is transcended, the greater its strength and vitality become. According to Maslow, you realize yourself in transcending the self in favor of the dynamic reality that arouses your interest.[1]

This phenomenon can be observed in the productive process in which genuine artists are entirely immersed. Lionel Trilling quotes two famous writers who testify to the self-forgetfulness that occurs in the midst of intense creativity. The first one is James Joyce, who declares, "The personality of the artist . . . finally refines itself out of existence, impersonalizes itself, so to speak." The second is T. S. Eliot, who avows, "The progress of an artist is a continual self-sacrifice, a continual extinction of personality."[2] One goes beyond one's ego thanks to a sort of "dis-identification"[3] or "de-coincidence" with that ego.[4]

Maslow draws attention to a central element in human nature that makes self-transcendence possible. Besides the Freudian superego, a form of conscience that flows from the internalizing of parental authority, there is what Maslow calls "intrinsic conscience," based on our perception of our own nature to be respected, our destiny to be discovered and fulfilled, our abilities to be developed and employed, the truth that we must not betray, and the courage called for in some situations.[5] From this important remark we should deduce, more explicitly than the author does, that we transcend ourselves not only by getting interested in reality, but also by identifying and choosing those aspects of reality that our intrinsic conscience sees as having to be valued, respected, and promoted.

For Maslow, human autonomy consists in taking account of this intrinsic conscience, allowing oneself to be led in the first

---

1. Maslow, *Psychology of Being*, 37 and 105.
2. Trilling, *Sincerity*, 7.
3. See Novak, "Attention," 501–9.
4. See Jullien, *Resources of Christianity*, "The Logic of De-coincidence," 56–71, and especially "What Is It to Be Alive?" 39–55. I think Jullien's view is supported by the distinctions between *psychē* (soul) and *zoē* (life) that he finds in the Evangelist John.
5. Maslow, *Psychology of Being*, 6–7.

place by interior motives, that is to say, by one's own nature and sense of personal vocation, goals, and talents. He emphasizes the necessity of maintaining a certain independence in the face of the environment and society, and in particular with respect to approval or disapproval, honors, rewards, accidental happenings, shocks, privations, and so on.

Maslow's intrinsic conscience accords with Walter Conn's construal of self-transcendence:

> Indeed, such realization of the self through transcendence is actually a form of self-fulfillment. However, it is a fulfillment of the fundamental desire for meaning, truth, value, and love characteristic of personal beings. While its fulfillment in self-transcendence brings a sense of peaceful happiness, the very nature of this basic human desire defies any self-centered striving for happiness through fulfillment.[6]

While insisting that each of us is autonomous, Maslow observes in the individual the capacity to become part of a greater whole. Rejecting a dichotomous manner of speaking, he unites in a hierarchical integration tendencies that are opposed to one another on a lower level but that are not opposed on a higher level: self-actualization and transcendence, awareness of intrinsic conscience and intense interest in exterior reality, inner ego-consistency and the desire to be part of a group wider than oneself, instinct and reason, heart and head, pleasure and duty, love of self and love of the other.[7] We shall examine some of these opposing tendencies.

The Role of Pleasure

No doubt because pleasure is by turns exalted and disparaged, it is hard to appreciate its true value. In a restricted sense, pleasure is physical. It accompanies the activity of the senses. Thus, we take pleasure in seeing, hearing, breathing, feeling, eating, drinking,

---

6. Conn, *The Desiring Self*, 72.
7. Maslow, *Psychology of Being*, 34–35, 91, 139–40, 180n1, and 212.

touching, moving, and sexually uniting. Usually, however, we understand pleasure in more general terms—as the enjoyment, interest, satisfaction, gratification, joy, or peace that precedes, accompanies, or follows a positive experience. We speak, for instance, of the pleasure of giving and receiving, of the pleasure of travel, or even, with Roland Barthes, of the pleasure of the text.[8]

Although physical pleasure undoubtedly exists, it cannot be attained in its pure state. Pleasure always takes on some kind of significance. The intellect situates pleasure in a meaningful context. The individual who pursues immediate pleasure often does so not only for enjoyment, but also to enhance his self-esteem thanks to the resoluteness, audacity, and creativity he employs in satisfying his needs. The human being does not find physical pleasure apart from the meaning he confers upon it. The film *Last Tango in Paris* illustrates the impossibility of experiencing a purely physical pleasure, which would imply forgetting all the rest.

The fact that we ascribe some meaning to a pleasure (even when we say we want it for itself) shows that we feel a need to justify it. To justify it is to place it in a context in which things take on meaning. When it acquires meaning, physical pleasure becomes allied with pleasure in the broader sense. For example, we derive pleasure from taking part in various sorts of meals, from lunch that is eaten quickly during the midday pause to dinner at an excellent restaurant, or a party at home, or a wedding banquet. The various significations attached to the meals complete the pleasure we get from eating well.[9]

For Aristotle, pleasure is something that accompanies a virtuous (or excellent) activity. Pleasure is neither the goal nor the objective of the activity; rather, it is an encouragement that flows from the activity. It is not the fruit, but the flower. The goal is the global meaning that one gives to one's life; the objective is the value of the activity itself, the good it represents. Pleasure is the joy felt in doing what has significance because it is estimable and well oriented. In accord with his Greek perspective, Aristotle

8. Barthes, *Pleasure*.
9. See Roy, *Embracing Desire*, 1–7.

finds deep satisfaction in the noble and beautiful character of the deed that is done.[10]

The objective and subjective sides of human action are thus conjoined. When a psychologically and morally healthy person says of an activity, "That interests me," she unites the objective and subjective aspects. She is concerned about both the value in question and the gratification that accompanies the experience. In a text that is worth citing at some length, the French philosopher Henri Bergson explains eloquently the living relationship that naturally exists between objectivity and subjectivity, creation and joy:

> Wherever there is joy, there is creation; the richer the creation, the deeper the joy. The mother beholding her child is joyous, because she is conscious of having created it, physically and morally. The merchant developing his business, the manufacturer seeing his industry prosper, are joyous—is it because money is gained and reputation acquired? No doubt, riches and social position count for much, but it is pleasures rather than joy that they bring; true joy, here, is the feeling of having started an enterprise which goes, of having brought something to life. Take exceptional joys—the joy of the artist who has realized his thought, the joy of the thinker who has made a discovery or invention. You may hear it said that these men work for glory and get their highest joy from the admiration they win. Profound error! We cling to praise and honours in the exact degree in which we are not sure of having succeeded. . . . But he who is sure, absolutely sure, of having produced a work which will endure and live, cares no more for praise and feels above glory, because he is a creator, because he knows it, because the joy he feels is the joy of a god.[11]

This joy is not the preserve of those who are exceptionally successful. Any person who believes in God and who tries to maintain a certain quality of life can participate in the divine creativity and experience of joy.

---

10. Aristotle, *Nicomachean Ethics*, book 1, §8, and book 10, §1–6.
11. Bergson, *Mind-Energy*, 29–30.

The Role of Effort

The role of pleasure, then, consists in accompanying and sustaining creative acts, which are sources of good. However, neither the apprehension of value nor the presence of pleasure is enough to guarantee that the required action will follow. Effort is also needed to exercise a function that completes that of pleasure.

When we are only barely motivated or are torn by contradictory motives, or when the value to be found can be attained only at the price of sacrificing intense pleasures, we act only with immense effort. And in some circumstances, strenuous effort is called for. Nonetheless, on the one hand, we are never well served by voluntarism, that is, by granting excessive importance to the will, as if its exertions might be meritorious in themselves. To avoid voluntarism, effort should be associated with and supported by pleasure understood in the broader sense. Moreover, obstacles ought not to be seen as detrimental but as opportunities to become a deeper and wiser person.

On the other hand, effort unavoidably involves tension. Viktor Frankl deplores the kind of education that dismisses effort:

> Today people are spared tension. First of all, this lack of tension is due to that loss of meaning which I describe as the existential vacuum, or the frustration of the will to meaning. . . . An education that is still based on the homeostasis theory is guided by the principle that as few demands as possible should be imposed upon young people. It is true that young people should not be subjected to excessive demands. However, we have also to consider the fact that, at least today, in the age of an affluent society, most people suffer too few demands rather than too many. The affluent society is an underdemanding society by which people are spared tension.[12]

---

12. Frankl, *The Will*, 44–45.

For Frankl, the homeostasis theory assumes that "man is basically concerned with maintaining or restoring an inner equilibrium, and to this end with the reduction of tensions."[13]

Freud speaks of the importance of knowing how to move from the pleasure principle—focused on what is immediate—to the reality principle—focused on the long term. He correctly considers the reality principle as safeguarding pleasure over a long stretch of time.[14] Effort becomes less arduous if one knows that it may lead to gratifications that matter more than the pleasures one must sacrifice. As Blaise Pascal wrote, "One does not give up pleasures except for other greater ones."[15]

All in all, pleasure is not meant to be an end in itself. Paradoxically, it is diminished when given priority over the good to be accomplished. Nevertheless, it is as sane and normal to want pleasure as to want the flower that signals the coming of the fruit, the good action. When a motivated person functions well, the satisfaction experienced is compensation for the effort made to accomplish the good. It is the sign of both the excellence of the person and the value of what is brought into being.

Unfortunately, some people imagine that the presence of pleasure discredits the authenticity of love. Cynics and idealists, whose positions are at opposite poles, nonetheless both mistakenly agree that there is no genuine love in an action that is pleasant. Cynics say, "We are egotists in every respect because in everything we do we seek only our own interest." Idealists make the claim that "True love is only what is costly, requires effort, and calls for much courage." The two groups have a negative understanding of pleasure, of the satisfaction one finds in performing good actions, and, in the last resort, of human nature itself. They cling to the false idea that love supposes absolute gratuity. However, they part company as the cynics are lucid, whereas the idealists find an escape in the opposition between the principles, which they admit very rarely

13. Frankl, *The Will*, 31.
14. Freud, *Civilization*, 26 and 29.
15. Pascal, *Oeuvres complètes*. 46.

work, and the conflict-free practical compromises, which seem inevitable for survival.

But even in the Holy Trinity, the divine Persons, while not having to acquire anything, enjoy one another in their exchanges. Furthermore, God has created human beings capable of entering into relationships where they both give and receive. We are so constituted that we cannot fail to obtain something whenever we love others sincerely and wisely.

The Hierarchy of Values

As quoted in chapter 2, Maslow points out that very few attain self-actualization. He offers two reasons to explain this disappointing fact. First, "the conviction that man's intrinsic nature is evil or dangerous"; and second, the fact that "humans no longer have strong instincts which tell them unequivocally what to do, when, where and how."[16] Insofar as the second reason is concerned, we may ask, are such "instincts" always constructive? Cultural or religious tendencies of a legalistic kind sometimes succeed in convincing and firmly guiding groups, and even whole societies. Still, one pays an excessive price for this, namely a diminution of critical rationality.

Notwithstanding the reservation I have just expressed, the problem posed by Maslow is a very real one. In extremely complex postindustrial societies, where the effects of our actions are more difficult to evaluate than they would be in an agrarian society, there is clearly a loss of objectivity. The kaleidoscopic screen of the mass media outruns our capacity for assimilation. The absence of a consensus regarding values and customs brings about a mixture of contradictory phenomena: rigidity and lawlessness, obstinacy and manipulation, intolerance and laissez faire. One way or the other, reflection and dialogue seem almost nonexistent. A large portion of the population loses sight of the importance of what takes place in the public sphere. People become alienated from their own work. In the private sphere, many try to compensate for

---

16. Maslow, *Psychology of Being*, 204.

the lack of satisfaction they find in their work by being absorbed in instant pleasures.

This does not mean that the private sphere remains inviolate. In his book *The Minimal Self*, Christopher Lasch rightly sees the "minimal or narcissistic self," which is characteristic of our time, as projected in "a world of mirrors, insubstantial images, illusions increasingly indistinguishable from reality." It is uncertain of itself, of the external reality, and of the boundaries between itself and that reality. Lasch argues that "the fantastic mass-produced images that shape our perceptions of the world" have brought about "the replacement of a reliable world of durable objects by a world of flickering images that make it harder and harder to distinguish reality from fantasy." The consequences are "submission to expert judgment, . . . distrust of their own capacity to make intelligent decisions."[17]

Part of the answer to this difficult problem lies in acquiring the hierarchy of values. Bernard Lonergan, a contemporary theologian, provides the following explanation of the scale of values.

> We may distinguish vital, social, cultural, personal and religious values in an ascending order. Vital values, such as health and strength, grace and vigor, normally are preferred to avoiding the work, privations, pains involved in acquiring, maintaining, restoring them. Social values, such as the good of order which conditions the vital values of the whole community, have to be preferred to the vital values of individual members of the community. Cultural values do not exist without the underpinning of vital and social values, but none the less they rank higher. Not on bread alone doth man live. Over and above mere living and operating, men have to find a meaning and value in their living and operating. It is the function of culture to discover, express, validate, criticize, correct, develop, improve such meaning and value. Personal value is the person in his self-transcendence, as loving and being loved, as originator of values in himself and in his milieu, as an inspiration and invitation to others to

---

17. Lasch, *The Minimal Self*, 30, 19, and 29.

do likewise. Religious values, finally, are at the heart of the meaning and value of man's living and man's world.[18]

For Lonergan, then, inferior values allow superior values to emerge in the following order: vital, social, cultural, personal, and religious. To realize one's potential amounts to actualizing one's values and skills, beginning with the vital ones of the body, including membership in communities and society, the quest for meaning in culture, excellent functioning as a person, and openness to the divine.

But how can we succeed in respecting this scale of preferences? In part, the answer is religious and dependent on perspectives and motives discussed in the following chapters. Another part of the response is philosophical; it has to do with the fact that the human being has the capacity to be truly interested in reality. Let us continue to take up the philosophical aspect of this question.

Intentionality and the Psyche

The Creator has implanted in us a fundamental dynamism that enables us to know, love, and transform. Following Brentano and Husserl, philosophers call this dynamism "intentionality," that is, the ability to tend toward (*in-tendere* in Latin), to open ourselves to reality. Now, this reality comprises not only things, animals, and humans around us, but also ourselves. To know, love, and transform ourselves is as spontaneous and legitimate as to know, love, and transform others. Therefore, our intentionality includes both self-realization and self-transcending toward reality. As I transcend myself, I realize myself as a loving subject.

Intentionality implies a twofold transcendence of self, as the two meanings of the verb "to transcend oneself" suggest. First, one transcends oneself by looking out of oneself in order to know and love persons and other beings as they are and not as one imagines or desires them to be. This requires the exercise of an exact and balanced judgment, carefully and correctly evaluating situations

---

18. Lonergan, *Method*, 32–33.

in order to achieve real good for other people. That is the *objective* aspect of intentionality, which consists in self-transcendence.

Human intentionality also wants to transcend itself in the sense of achieving excellence. And here we have the *subjective* aspect of the same dynamism, which amounts to self-realization. Every individual endowed with a certain measure of vitality possesses in some way a taste for excellence. Once basic needs are satisfied, as Maslow points out, the vital person desires to face more significant challenges, which are more satisfying, give meaning to daily life, and allow her to grow as a human being.[19]

To achieve self-realization, one must take into account both one's intentionality and one's psyche. Intentionality is the source of questioning and reflection. It is open to the external world, seeking to understand and evaluate it. It looks to exact knowledge, well-founded value judgments, and the discernment of lines of action that respect other people in their environment. This is to say that intentionality has a moral dimension in its deepest sense. While intentionality is the principle of unlimited opening to the whole of reality, the psyche appears as the principle of limitation. Since the psyche is in touch with our bodily needs, it carries out the function of mediating them to our intentionality by way of affects and images.[20]

On the one hand, without a healthy psyche, intentionality tends to be disembodied, cold, legalistic, willful, and even destructive. When people cannot count on a sound psyche, their behavior gets distorted, despite their good intentions. On the other hand, if intentionality operates as it should, it strives to establish an alliance and an equilibrium with the psyche. By making wise decisions regarding one's lifestyle, intentionality helps the psyche to flourish in a relatively harmonious atmosphere enabling positive perceptions and feelings. Moreover, the psyche can accept frustrations, which intentionality should negotiate—not impose in a

---

19. Maslow, *Psychology of Being*, 25. For a more thorough analysis, see Roy, *Transcendent Experiences*, 151–56.

20. My understanding of intentionality and psyche is dependent upon Doran, *Psychic Conversion*, 28–29.

dictatorial manner. Thus, in any well-balanced person there is a dynamic tension between intentionality and the psyche.

Love of Self and Love of Neighbor

The philosophical and psychological principles set forth in this chapter lead to the conclusion that far from excluding each other, love of self and love for the other are complementary.[21]

We have seen in chapters 1 and 2 that neither altruism nor egoism promotes self-realization. In fact, on the one hand, to renounce one's pleasure systematically in favor of others' pleasure constitutes a sacrifice that inevitably engenders frustration, attempts to obtain some compensation, resentment, and even hostility. On the other hand, consistently putting one's own pleasure before that of others brings only bitter satisfaction to even the least lucid individual.

Paradoxically, selflessness and egotism have the same roots: both are misguided ways of valuing oneself, either by one's misplaced generosity or by one's numerous acts and pleasures. In each case, an important aspect of the self is ignored. A self-denying person ignores his wishes by not acknowledging his legitimate needs, his valuable ideas, his profound aspirations, and the unique way he could realize himself as a human being. An egotist ignores that inclination in himself which desires to love the other for what she is, and to promote in society values that are independent of his own immediate interests. Both the one who systematically sacrifices himself and the one who remains consistently self-absorbed are victims of mistaken strategies, associated with false notions of what it means to love others and oneself.[22]

A sound philosophy of love rests on intentionality. It is manifested in the tendency to ask appropriate questions: Who is this

---

21. On the compatibility between self-love and benevolence, see Butler, *Five Sermons*, sermons 4 and 5, "Upon the Love of our Neighbor" [= sermons 11 and 12 of the complete edition, titled *Fifteen Sermons Preached at the Rolls Chapel*].

22. More will be said on love for others and love for oneself in chapter 6.

person? What are the problems and procedures of this group? Is my information correct? Is the action I contemplate worthwhile? Will this act prove to be a good means to the end? What attitudes are suitable in this situation? This kind of questioning shows that it is natural to pay attention to reality, to people, to the good to be sought, and to steps to be planned.

Now, the reality that must be understood, loved, and transformed includes the self as well as the other. Therefore, to love is neither always to concentrate totally on others nor always to be centered on oneself; it is to alternate between these two complementary operations. The alternation ought not to be misconceived as an alternation in terms of loving: one does not sometimes love others and sometimes love oneself. Rather, the alternation is a matter of accents in attentiveness. On the one hand, we must turn toward the external reality that requires commitment, toward the true good of other people, toward the institutions and practices which sustain a just and harmonious social life. On the other hand, we must face our own reality, know our potential, discover the basic line of our destiny, and choose activities that are suitable to our personality.[23]

Erich Fromm points out what we can gain from knowing how to give:

> In the very act of giving, I experience my strength, my wealth, my power. This experience of heightened vitality and potency fills me with joy. I experience myself as overflowing, spending, alive, hence as joyous. Giving is more joyous than receiving, not because it is a deprivation, but because in the act itself of giving lies the expression of my vitality.[24]

Although it is insightful, Fromm's description of the pleasure received in giving does not go far enough. This pleasure is really more than the agreeable feeling of one's power, vitality, and wealth. The satisfaction derived from giving is deeper because it is also

23. In Vacek, *Love*. The author offers a balanced treatment of self-love and love for others, which is more detailed than the one I give here.

24. Fromm, *Art of Loving*, 18–19.

linked to intentionality—viewing the other as different from me, identifying the needs and desires of the person I love, and responding with both affection and intelligence to the profound value that I discern in the other. This is precisely what sincere love wants for its partner: that the other might taste in turn the joy of paying attention to me, truly understanding me, and loving me with his whole heart and mind. For the sake of oneself and the other, there is an objective interest in inviting the other to grow in love.

And yet, despite the irreplaceable role that it plays in sustaining and rewarding the effort that love requires, this joy is more than enthusiasm aroused by functioning well, even in love. Joy derives from a good act, and the act is seen to be good if its object is worthwhile. If one attends to what intentionality at its best is really pursuing, one notices that love finds its *raison d'être* beyond the satisfaction of loving. To love and be loved is to want to love and be loved *because it is good*, because it fits within a human relationship. Love is justified first and above all by virtue of the good it seeks.

In interpersonal love, the growth of the people involved is paramount. The satisfaction of loving accompanies the actualization of this good and contributes to the development of each person. Effort is seen as an ally of satisfaction, while both effort and satisfaction are subordinated to the emergence of this good. It is not natural to love and help people first and above all in view of the joy one will derive from it. On the contrary, to be fully human consists in welcoming with gratitude the joy of loving and of acting justly because that joy helps me to love and act justly. From the Aristotelian viewpoint adopted in this chapter, the pleasure of contributing to the advancement of a person or a group is obtained as a consequence inseparably linked to that good.

To return to the rather optimistic quotation from Erich Fromm, it should be mentioned that he does not take into account the dramatic situations in which most human beings often find themselves. In times of suffering, many find it extremely difficult not to break down. They need to draw upon resources that are usually considered religious. In the trials of life, love develops and takes on its full meaning only if it is taken up into a larger whole of a transcendent kind, which makes it possible to cope with the question of evil. This broader context will be sketched in the following chapters.

4

The Radical Gospel
Historical Setting

What we find in the New Testament on self-realization appears to be totally opposed to the humanistic plan for self-development. It is a matter of what the exegete Thaddée Matura calls "gospel radicalism," defined as "the most absolute requirements of Christian existence." Matura understands "radical" to mean what goes against ordinary wisdom, "what departs from habitual behavior and customs, what is extreme, hard, trenchant, abrupt and demanding."[1]

Gospel radicalism is incarnated in many forms: to be poor, chaste, faithful to one's marriage partner, to become a wanderer dependent on the hospitality of others, to choose Christ and the Gospel over one's intimates, to castrate oneself for the kingdom of heaven, to renounce power, to welcome the alien, to be open to sinners and those excluded from society, to forgive seventy times seven times, to do good to one's enemies, to take the last place, to accept insults, calumnies, arrest, trial, loss of material goods, torture, and death.

---

1. Matura, *Suivre Jésus*, 23–24.

It is impossible, of course, for any one person to respond to all these demands at the same time. Some of them are, in fact, incompatible—for instance, fidelity to one's marriage partner and celibacy for the kingdom. On the other hand, how could one be a Christian without manifesting in one's life some form of this radicalism? In church history, each generation of believers has been creative in this regard. Every period, every Christian community, and every person has been invited to identify the forms of radicalism that should be actualized in the following of Christ. Sometimes the disciples of Jesus have become radical as a result of having taken bold initiatives; sometimes they have become so simply by having consented to the implications of their religious commitment.

The New Testament asks believers to perform costly acts, to adopt courageous attitudes, and not to shun painful situations. However, it would be a mistake to think that these actions, attitudes, and sufferings have religious value in and of themselves. To understand why the Gospel is so revolutionary, we must examine its various contexts.[2]

Mission and Opposition

One of these contexts is that of mission. Sent by Jesus, the disciples became itinerants who traveled with as few goods as possible. Thus, they were dependent, because they needed the hospitality of those who did not share their Christian faith. "Take no gold, or silver, or copper in your belts, no bag for your journey, or two tunics, or sandals, or a staff; for laborers deserve their food" (Matt 10:9–10). These missionaries are the "little ones" spoken of in Matthew 10:42 and with whom Jesus identifies himself in Matthew 25:31–46. It is to them that kindly non-Christians gave food and drink; it is they who were welcomed when they were strangers, who were clothed when they were naked, and who were cared for when they were ill; it is they who were visited in prison.

2. My reading of the beatitudes has been heavily influenced by Dupont, *Les béatitudes*.

The content of their preaching caused hostility and created a situation of opposition, resulting in conflicts, insults, calumnies, arrests, trials, flagellations, and death (Matt 10:16–20). Poverty for the sake of the Gospel is explained by these two situations—itinerancy and opposition. A disciple was poor either because he left his possessions behind in order to go from village to village proclaiming the good news or because his goods were seized by adversaries who rejected the Christian message. Moreover, when certain members of the Jewish or pagan community recognized Jesus as the savior and others did not, the new Christians sometimes lost the love of their close relatives. Thus came painful divisions and denunciations within families and towns (Matt 10:21–22, 34–39).

This complex situation of preaching and conflict can be seen in the life of St. Paul, who felt responsible for and united with all human beings, since God calls every person to be part of the Body of Christ. Nothing can be understood about Paul without first grasping his missionary desire to spread the Word that liberates worldwide and to provide support to all who are in the process of conversion and transformation. He explained this several times, notably in chapter 2 of the first letter to the Thessalonians. He wrote that he did not seek to please people or to receive honors. His dedication to the recipients of his letter was complete. "So deeply do we care for you that we are determined to share with you not only the gospel of God but also our own selves, because you have become very dear to us" (1 Thess 2:8).

His attention was focused on one thing: making known "the good news," "the word of God" (1 Thess 2:2–9, 13). His motivation was eschatological; it looked toward the community of the last days. "For what is our hope or joy or crown of boasting before our Lord Jesus at his coming? Is it not you? Yes, you are our glory and joy!" (1 Thess 2:19–20).

Invitation to the Marginal

Ending the marginalization of those in Israel who were considered impure constitutes another context of self-transcendence. The evangelists saw Jesus not as a prophet who kept himself pure by avoiding contact with the unclean but rather as the Holy One of God, who cured them by communicating his own purity to them. The first stage of salvation brought by Jesus consisted in bringing back "the lost sheep of the house of Israel" (Matt 10:6; 15:24) in order to restore the whole nation to its pristine unity. Note the list of those who enter the kingdom first or to whom the good news must be preached first: the sick, the dead, and the lepers (Matt 10:8); the blind, the lame, the lepers, the deaf, the dead, and the poor (Matt 11:5; Luke 7:22); the poor, the captives, the blind, the oppressed, and all those who will profit by a "year of the Lord's favor" (Luke 4:18–19); the poor, the crippled, the blind, and the lame (Luke 14:21).

Giving priority to the "unclean" could not help but raise problems for Jesus. The Pharisees and the scribes complained, "This fellow welcomes sinners and eats with them" (Luke 15:2). The difficulty came from the fact that his welcome was not preceded by any request for purification. For instance, in the case of Zacchaeus (Luke 19:1–10), Jesus did not immediately require acknowledgment of sin, and he himself initiated the contact. He also took the initiative in inviting himself to dinner at the home of a public sinner, thus fulfilling a deep aspiration on the part of Zacchaeus, who "was trying to see who Jesus was." In sharing a meal with this sinner, who was excluded by the religious authorities, Jesus offered him the possibility of communion with God. The incomparable presence of Jesus—rather, of God, who saves through the humanity of Jesus—gave Zacchaeus the motivation he needed to be converted.[3]

During the Pauline mission to the pagans, a similar problem arose. Many Jews, even among those who believed in Jesus, did not admit that Christianity (which was then viewed as a branch of Judaism) could exempt from the Mosaic regulations pagans who had been converted to Christ. The openness that Jesus had shown to sinners who were Israelites, and the welcome he accorded to

---

3. On this basic option by Jesus, see Roy, *God*, chap. 2, section entitled "The Kind of God that Jesus Represents."

pagans who had not embraced Judaism, furnished other reasons for some leaders to attack the first Christians. We find an echo in the parable of the workers in the vineyard (Matt 20:1–16). Projecting onto God a human idea of justice which is not sufficiently aware of divine generosity, certain Jews who had worked for centuries in the vineyard of the Lord found it unreasonable that the recently arrived pagans should receive the same wages. Furthermore, Jesus did not hide the fact that the blunted spirituality of Israel would have disquieting results: "The last will be first, and the first will be last."

Stating that the kingdom of God was open to the unclean and to the pagans, Jesus aroused opposition in those who believed that the frontiers of religious purity and moral observance should be impenetrable to such people. It was not that Jesus abolished these frontiers. On the contrary, his calls for repentance make clear that he did not practice any complicity with sin. Far from diminishing the difference between good and evil, he accentuated it. But having taken this difference to an extreme (in the Sermon on the Mount), Jesus showed that the kindness of God cancels out evil as he drew near to sinners and loved them deeply. This radicalism on the part of Jesus had a way of frightening the just. How, indeed, can one love sinners without collusion? How can one find the strength to enter this dangerous and unsatisfactory path? Fears like these prompted many to reject the message of Jesus.

Moreover, the priority Jesus accorded to the poor and his announcement of a reversal of social situations naturally led most of the rich to perceive the good news as bad news. "How hard it is for those who have wealth to enter the kingdom of God! Indeed, it is easier for a camel to go through the eye of a needle than for someone who is rich to enter the kingdom of God" (Luke 18:24–25).

Luke points out that certain Pharisees, who loved money, made fun of the warnings of Jesus about the incompatibility of serving God and wealth (16:10–15). While Jesus did not condemn the possession of money, he nevertheless denounced the prestige and the illusory security associated with money, as can be seen in the episode of the poor widow (21:1–4), the parable of Lazarus and the rich man (16:19–31), and the story of the wealthy landowner who amassed considerable stores of grain just before his death (12:13–26).

It is easy to understand why the priority Jesus gave to the marginalized, pagans, and the poor aroused the indignation of the orthodox and constituted a challenge for the disciples.

Relationships within Communities

Relationships within Christian communities constitute another context of self-transcendence. The disciples were invited to prefer the last place to the first (Luke 14:7–11). Unlike the heads of nations, religious leaders were told not to make their power felt, but instead to become the servants of others (Matt 20:20–28). The greatest in the kingdom, Jesus said, will be the little one, the child, the youngest, the one who serves at table (Matt 18:1–5; 19:13–15; Luke 22:24–27).

Christian brothers and sisters should be concerned about the sheep that has gone astray; they ought to correct one another and pardon one another from the bottom of their hearts—not seven times, but seventy times seven times (Matt 18:10–35). Among the petitions in the "Our Father," this duty of forgiving is the only one that Jesus returns to and insists upon (Matt 6:9–15). Its importance is thereby highlighted.

Matthew emphasizes another situation where love requires some delicacy: not to occasion the fall of a little one, while taking care not to fall oneself (Matt 18:6–9). Paul discusses this problem in chapter 8 of his first letter to the Corinthians. On the one hand, he defends the freedom of the Christian to eat food sacrificed to idols. Those who believe in the one God know well, of course, that idols do not exist outside the minds of those who venerate them. On the other hand, Paul points out that, for the weak, an occasion of falling might be caused by this freedom. Paul concludes, "Therefore, if food is a cause of their falling, I will never eat meat, so that I may not cause one of them to fall" (1 Cor 8:13). It is in this context that he urges his fellow Christians: "Do not seek your own advantage, but that of others" (1 Cor 10:24; see v. 33).

Suffering, Attitudes, and Behavior

Another form of radicalism consists in the sufferings that Jesus invited his followers to undertake. Addressed directly to disciples ("Blessed are *you*") who found themselves in difficult situations, the beatitudes in Luke's Gospel proclaim that those are blessed who are poor, hungry, mourning, hated by others, rejected, insulted, and defamed for the sake of the Son of Man (compare with 1 Cor 4:9-13). The beatitudes and the curses (Luke 6:20-26), as well as Mary's canticle (Luke 1:46-55), announce a reversal of fortunes linked to the advent of a new world.

In Matthew 5:3-12, the beatitudes have more to do with attitudes and behavior. There, Jesus proclaims blessed the poor in spirit, the meek, those who are waiting to be comforted, those who hunger and thirst for justice (namely to accomplish God's will), the merciful, the pure of heart, the peacemakers, and those who are persecuted for the sake of justice.

The six antitheses that follow (Matt 5:21-48) urge the disciple to go as far as possible in respecting others: not to become angry with one's brother, nor insult him, but rather to be reconciled with him; not to look at another man's wife to desire her, but to take even drastic measures to avoid sin; not to repudiate one's wife or marry the rejected wife of another; not to swear at all, but to keep one's word; not to resist an evildoer, to turn the other cheek, to give the thief one's coat and to give generously to those who ask; to love one's enemies, to pray for one's persecutors; and not to be content with loving only one's brothers and sisters and those who love in return. Matthew's antitheses uncover that which people would ignore: the roots of violence, be it against one's brother, one's wife, the person that one sexually desires, the contender in court, the enemy, the persecutor, or the stranger.

Commenting on the Sermon on the Mount, Ronald Rolheiser points out: "We can keep all the commandments and be just to our neighbor without having to love our enemies or having to forgive one another. Justice is predicated on fairness, an eye for an eye, and that of itself does not demand forgiveness or that we love our enemies."[4]

Finally, passages from the Gospels that do not form part of such organized wholes also point to radical acts to be accomplished. Thus, in response to the question "Who is my neighbor?" Luke 10:29–37 cites the example of the good Samaritan, a foreigner who acted as a neighbor to the man who had been robbed, beaten, and left for dead on the road from Jerusalem to Jericho. In the same way, Jesus suggests to a person giving a banquet that his guests be the poor, the crippled, the lame, and the blind, who will not be able to repay; these will, in fact, be the ones whom God will bring together at the great banquet in the kingdom (Luke 14:12–24). Or again, following the requirement of conjugal fidelity, repeated by Matthew in chapter 19, Jesus evokes the possibility of celibacy for the sake of the kingdom of heaven.

We have sketched numerous forms of Christian radicalism found in various situations in the New Testament. It remains for us to complete this inventory by asking what meaning such radicalism might have in our present world.

---

4. Rolheiser, *Sacred Fire*, 154.

5

The Radical Gospel
An Interpretation

Having drawn attention to the numerous forms of radicalism found in the New Testament (especially in the Synoptic Gospels and St. Paul), we must go further and attempt to answer the following questions: What motivation makes radicalism possible? To whom does Jesus address his calls for self-denial? How can one live out nonresistance and forgiveness?

Motivation

Certain expressions that appear in the context of self-denial reveal the motivation that underlies radicalism. When Jesus urged his disciples to undertake difficult acts of renunciation, he gave the following reasons: "because of my name" (Matt 10:22); "for my sake" (10:39); "for my sake, and for the sake of the gospel" (Mark 8:35); "for the sake of the kingdom of heaven" (Matt 19:12). In the face of what Jesus represented, the good news that he proclaimed, and the kingdom of God that was present in his person and in his actions, the radical words he spoke find their context. It was the urgency of the desire to devote oneself to the kingdom of God that explains the fact that the disciple had nowhere to lay his head and renounced going first to bury his father or to say farewell to members of his household (Luke 9:57–62).

Exegetes point out that the kingdom of God is the leitmotif of the Gospels, that this theme is found in all the literary genres, and that all the other motifs are clarified by this theme.[1] The message Jesus brought is the "good news" (the gospel), closely linked to the coming of the kingdom of God (Mark 1:14–15). The good news is announced first and foremost to the poor (Matt 11:5; Luke 4:18), as Isaiah predicted (Isa 61:1). The poor, be it noted, include tax collectors and sinners, who recognize more easily their need for a physician than people in good health (Matt 9:9–13). The sinful woman, because she is aware that her numerous sins have been forgiven, shows much love (Luke 7:35–50). Thanks to their faith, public sinners such as tax collectors and prostitutes will precede the priests and the elders into the kingdom of God (Matt 21:23–32). They welcome with more truthfulness and depth the healing and liberation offered by Jesus.

Moreover, the kingdom implies the tearing down of walls and barriers that separate human beings, often in the name of God. Such was the case with Israel in the time of Jesus. He himself went out to the rejected and touched those who were afflicted with ills attributed at that time to the presence of various demons. When the Pharisees claimed that Jesus cast out devils by the prince of devils, Jesus replied that it was impossible for the house of Satan to be thus divided against itself. He added, "But if it is by the Spirit of God that I cast out demons, then the kingdom of God has come to you" (Matt 12:28). The kingdom of God is realized, then, in the action of Jesus. His cures indicate that the kingdom is already present. In the same way, one can view acts of radicalism as signs of the kingdom. As Matthew 19:12 suggests, certain believers decide to be celibates "for the sake of the kingdom of heaven."

There was strong opposition raised in reaction to the proclamation and realization of the kingdom of God. Jesus was the first to experience enormous opposition to his message and his way of

---

1. See Gourgues, *Jésus*, 27.

life. Indeed, his arrest, condemnation, and crucifixion issued from the rejection of that message and way of life. However, insofar as Christians misunderstand the message and fail to imitate its practice, the world honors them. On the other hand, as soon as they take seriously the radicalism of the Gospel, they become the target of defamation, and means are taken to overcome their influence:

> If the world hates you, be aware that it hated me before it hated you. If you belonged to the world, the world would love you as its own. Because you do not belong to the world, but I have chosen you out of the world—therefore the world hates you. Remember the word that I said to you, "Servants are not greater than their master." If they persecuted me, they will persecute you. (John 15:18–20)

Radicalism is motivated by the desire to imitate this master whom one admires, to resemble more and more this friend and brother, who shows the way that leads to life.

The nobleness of Jesus, which believers can imitate, amounts to defying the consequences of one's commitment. It consists in maintaining one's orientation and in declaring that it is willed by God. It means going so far as to assert that there is no salvation outside of this way (Acts 4:12). It is to proclaim courageously the necessity of conversion for all, from the smallest to the greatest. Thence comes the deadly antipathy of those who do not believe Jesus was the mouthpiece of God. They think that the established order is threatened by the inflexible allegiance of his disciples to "truth," and they fear that attempts may be made to overthrow an unjust state of affairs which benefit those who oppose the Gospel.

Jesus proclaimed, "It is more blessed to give than to receive" (Acts 20:35). Yet giving is associated with suffering. Reflecting on the life of Jesus, one cannot fail to be struck by his heroism. Unfortunately, many are content to admire it from a distance, without wondering about its source. The foundation of this heroism is the coming of the kingdom. Because God comes to reign, a new horizon appears, and great things become possible. Faith in the kingdom of God, which was realized in the action of Jesus, led both Jesus and his disciples to strikingly radical acts, attitudes, situations, and sufferings.

Judged abnormal by all purely human standards, these actions take on a convincing meaning in the Christian context. It is a matter of making visible the immense generosity of God, which is the substance of the great charter of the kingdom. As Helmut Thielicke emphasizes, in the logic of the New Testament, the divine gift precedes the radical commands: "we are not given something to do without first being given something."[2] He explains:

> The sermon on the Mount says to us: a future has been *given* to you. . . . In the name of that future we can afford to be radical and absolutely straight, without allowing ourselves to be pushed off on the diagonals of the parallelogram of power or to tack on a zigzag course. In other words: first comes the future and then the unconditional demand, the straight line, the right course—and not the other way around.[3]

Given this extraordinary future, the believer wants to express the kindness, the tenderness, the mercy, the unparalleled love of God for all human beings. By becoming one with the least interesting, the most deprived, and the most hardened of human beings, she *takes the initiative* of showing the signs of the kingdom. In order to share with others the Father's extravagant love as manifested by Jesus, she is ready to accept actions, attitudes, situations, and sufferings that seem irrational, humanly speaking. All this is to be explained by the fact that the disciples have received the light of faith, which allows them to look at people and events through the eyes of Jesus.

Faith in the reality of the kingdom, then, makes possible great love for one's neighbor. This same faith, likewise, allows one to accept evil. The cross of Jesus sheds light on the failures, defeats, sufferings, and absurdities one undergoes. Any negative experience can become fruitful if it is lived with love, in union with Jesus.

---

2. Thielicke, *Life*, xiii.
3. Thielicke, *Life*, xiv.

> Very truly, I tell you, unless a grain of wheat falls into the earth and dies, it remains just a single grain; but if it dies, it bears much fruit. Those who love their life lose it, and those who hate their life in this world will keep it for eternal life. (John 12:24-25)

One finds here the religious motive, which sustains the gift of self for others. One is willing to sacrifice oneself for the Gospel, for the people one loves, and even for one's enemies, because one believes it will contribute to the salvation of the world. Gospel radicalism finds its ground and dynamism in the very way God wants to liberate humankind.

Psychologically, this self-gift amounts to what Gabriel Marcel called *disponibilité* ("availability"). In the wake of Marcel, Paul Ricoeur comments: "Availability is the key that opens self-constancy to the dialogic structure established by the Golden Rule." I can then see the other as "someone who is counting on me and making self-constancy a response to this expectation. To a large extent, it is not to disappoint or betray this expectation that I make maintaining my first intention the theme of a redoubled intention: the intention not to change my intention."[4] This disposition constitutes the structure of promise and faithfulness.

Those to Whom the Message Is Addressed

To whom are the appeals to radicalism addressed? The vocabulary indicates that a good number of such challenges are addressed to all Christians: "all," "whoever," "the disciples," "the crowd." Precepts of a general nature are valid for everyone because they sum up what the particular precepts set forth in detail. Thus, every disciple must follow Jesus, carry one's cross, and lose one's life. However, although this condition is common to all, there are countless ways of enacting it.

That is why many radical acts are not imposed on all; they variously apply to particular situations and circumstances. Foreign

---

4. Ricoeur, *Oneself*, 268, see 165.

missionaries, for example, are itinerant, renounce material goods, and live far from their families. Also, persecutions occur regularly in the course of the history of the church. In some countries, for example, not belonging to the ruling party may mean that one is deprived of interesting studies and a promising career; dissent can result in incarceration in a psychiatric hospital or prison, forced labor, or exile. Activities on behalf of human rights can usher in a situation where an individual is molested, beaten, or tortured. In regimes of the extreme Left as well as of the extreme Right, many Christians of living faith have paid dearly for their commitment to truth and justice.

Nevertheless, an adequate interpretation of the radical Gospel rules out a number of alternatives. First, the Sermon on the Mount is not a set of laws literally imposed on everyone. As was pointed out at the beginning of chapter 4, some of those laws happen to be incompatible with others. It would be a mistake to think that they are binding precepts for all Christians. In keeping with this inadequate construal, they would be supernatural commands as universal as Kant's categorical imperatives, based on practical reason.[5] By contrast, here are François de Sales's wise considerations on the subject:

> Each individual Christian is unable and would be ill advised to try to practise all the counsels. . . . We have the sufficient love for all the counsels if we are devoted in keeping those suited to our state. . . . Heroic virtue is not usually commanded, only counselled. So that if on occasion we meet with the obligation of practising it, the circumstances are unusual or rare enough to make such practice necessary for preserving God's grace.[6]

Second, a similar error consists in stating, after Luther, that the pronouncements of Jesus are at once morally inescapable and unattainable. As such, their role would be to expose the believers' sinfulness, so that they may give up their confidence in human

---

5. Kant, *Grounding*, 402, 421, 429–34, 440, and 444 (marginal numbers).

6. de Sales, *Love*, 336–37 and 339. This ninth chapter in book 8 gives several instances of when a particular counsel must be implemented.

works and entrust themselves to divine grace.[7] In partial agreement and disagreement with Luther, I would maintain that *with the grace* imparted by Christ, the requirements of the radical Gospel are in a great measure applicable. Thus, Thomas Aquinas stresses the action of grace as all-important: "The letter, even of the Gospel, would kill, unless there were the inward presence of the healing grace of faith."[8]

Third, Max Weber drives a wedge between an ethics of conviction (*Gesinnungsethik*), illustrated by the Sermon on the Mount, and an ethics of responsibility (*Verantwortungsethik*), represented by the practice of those who must run human affairs. This highly influential German sociologist maintains that there is total opposition between the former, essentially pacifist, and the latter, based on violence (or the violent squelching of violence). Being idealistic, "acosmic," and confined to the realm of personal relations, the first kind of ethics can be adopted only by saints and may serve as an inspiration. Weber's resigned acceptance of the second kind of ethics, the only kind viable on the collective plane, follows from his tacit assumption that there is no divine grace operative in the people who make political decisions. All the same, he acknowledges the fact that sometimes politicians combine conviction with responsibility—which seems to rebuke the fundamental opposition he has set between the two kinds of ethics.[9]

Having dispensed with grace, Weber offers a secularized version of Luther's view, with its separation of the inner man from the outer man. Weber rightly sees, however, how self-deceptive is the attitude of those who cultivate generous feelings and good intentions at the neglect of social analysis and realistic behavior. The radicalism of the Gospel has nothing to do with a vague romantic inspiration that would occasionally call for impotent forms of social protest.

Fourth, another way of bypassing Matthew's Sermon on the Mount—and the even more demanding Luke's Sermon on the

---

7. Luther, *Christian Liberty*, 11–12.
8. Aquinas, *Summa Theologiae*, I-II, q. 106, a. 2.
9. Weber, *Politics*, esp. 45–55.

Plain—is to declare that they are an obsolete ethics, an ethics that was viable only during the period of eschatological crisis that followed the resurrection of Jesus. In contrast to the first disciples of Jesus, who expected an imminent end of the world and thus could afford being heroic for a little while, we would be entitled to see the words of Jesus as beautifully expressing a mere ideal. Inspirational though it could be, this dream would never be concretized into practical decisions, particularly over a long period of time.

Fifth, contrary to what Aquinas teaches, it is an anachronism to see the pressing appeals for self-abnegation found in the Gospels as counsels specifically addressed to members of religious communities whose life is more perfect by being structured along the requirements of obedience, poverty, and chastity.[10] The New Testament nowhere suggests a distinction between precepts for all believers and counsels for the religious. Countless lay Christians have adopted forms of radicality that are different from religious life and no less demanding. Furthermore, the New Testament's ethics is not elitist: all are called to practice its exigencies, with a mixture of success and failure.

If we look closely at the details of the radical Gospel, we can observe that certain of Jesus' appeals—such as love, forgiveness, and purity of the heart—are obviously universal. Other appeals are particular: for instance, celibacy: "Let anyone accept this who can" is the challenge Jesus flings down in Matthew 19:12. The command not to divorce one's wife is also particular. After all, Jesus never urges anyone to get married; therefore, his precept about not divorcing applies only to those who have bound themselves to another person out of love (see Matt 19:9). Whether universal or particular, however, these radical points all reflect real practices in New Testament times. It is necessary, then, to envisage them, in all their diversity, as the many *possibilities* offered by the kingdom—possibilities that become *actualities* thanks to divine grace. "The content of these requirements is often clear-cut and definite; the

---

10. Aquinas, *Summa Theologiae*, II–II, q. 186, a. 1 and a. 2.

way to live them in the concrete is left, as a disquieting challenge, to creative invention."[11]

For example, what are the requirements regarding the sharing of goods? Such sharing seems to be required of everyone, at least in the sense that according to the tradition of most churches, Christians should give a part of their income to their parish, which must then care for the poor. But certain groups go so far as to hold all their goods in common. The Acts of the Apostles (2:44-45 and 4:32-37) recounts how this integral sharing of goods allowed the leaders to distribute them according to the needs of the members of the community, so that no one was in want. This is a possibility offered by the kingdom, which quite a few perceive as a goal to be realized in their own lives. To the rich young man who had kept all the commandments, Jesus said: "If you wish to be perfect, go, sell your possessions, and give the money to the poor, and you will have treasure in heaven; then come, follow me" (Matt 19:21). Note the appeal to personal freedom: "If you wish to be perfect." This appeal meets a desire to do or to be more: "What do I still lack?" (Matt 19:20). But there are times when the desire can prove too weak: "He went away grieving, for he had many possessions" (Matt 19:22).

Similar differences are found concerning commitment to the mission. Although not all Christians are called to be apostles in the way that St. Paul was, all should offer and direct their daily actions to facilitate, directly or indirectly, the conversion to Jesus Christ. This collaboration in the Christian mission is carried out in interpersonal relationships and in the physical and organizational activities that support them. A hierarchy of values unites communion with God, human relations, and the rest of our activities, so that in the economy of the incarnation nothing is despised. What is asked of all Christians is to act wholeheartedly and bring a high quality to their daily tasks, as humble and routine as they may be.

The Gospel bids us to do more than what is strictly necessary and to follow appeals that lead in different directions. For example, in prayer, acceptance of intimacy with God is a costly way of living

11. Matura, *Le radicalisme*, 198.

radicalism. "Whenever you pray, go into your room and shut the door and pray to your Father who is in secret; and your Father who sees in secret will reward you" (Matt 6:6). In a world where people are accustomed to receiving strong daily doses of sensory stimulation, it takes a courageous resolve to accept the austerity of solitude and silence.

A radical stance is also displayed in commitment to social justice. Postindustrial societies tend to isolate and overlook those whose personality and lifestyle do not manifest the general mood of optimism: members of the lower economic classes, the unemployed, those on public assistance, people with disabilities, the ill, the elderly, the dying, and so forth. To break down this barrier requires sacrifice. To respect profoundly the small as well as the great, to put those who are in dire necessity ahead of those with less need, to struggle against attitudes based on contempt and prejudice—all this runs counter to what most human beings think and do. Moreover, if someone is serious about staying informed about economic injustice and its causes, and about putting pressure on political leaders through various channels of communication, this individual becomes unpopular. Pope John Paul II brought criticism upon himself when he called attention to the debts of poor nations and the exploitation of the Third World by capitalist countries.

Gospel radicalism is thus a risky and less traveled road. It is "the Way of God" (Acts 18:26). One must go forward with confidence and inventiveness in following him who is "the way, and the truth, and the life" (John 14:6). It is for each person to discern, among the many types of radicalism that the kingdom makes possible, which ones are suited to one's nature and circumstances. Each person and each Christian community must determine for themselves what reality corresponds to the call of God.

Nonresistance and Forgiveness

To complete this discussion of radicalism, let us examine two often misunderstood passages of the Sermon on the Mount. The first of these passages concerns nonresistance:

> But I say to you, Do not resist an evildoer. But if anyone strikes you on the right cheek, turn the other also; and if anyone wants to sue you and take your coat, give your cloak as well; and if anyone forces you to go one mile, go also the second mile. Give to everyone who begs from you, and do not refuse anyone who wants to borrow from you. (Matt 5:39-42)

Yet Jesus himself seems *not* to have put into practice what he recommends. Struck by one of the high priest's guards, he did not turn the other cheek, but replied, "If I have spoken wrongly, testify to the wrong. But if I have spoken rightly, why do you strike me?" (John 18:23). And when Paul, the great apostle of Jesus Christ, was struck on the order of the high priest, he did not mince his words: "God will strike you, you whitewashed wall! Are you sitting there to judge me according to the law, and yet in violation of the law you order me to be struck?" (Acts 23:3).

No intelligible interpretation of this Gospel text can be made if we consider the precept universal. The clear practice of Jesus and Paul contradicts it. But one can view that saying of Jesus as a possibility of the kingdom, to be discerned and put into practice whenever necessary. At certain moments in interpersonal relationships and in the life of groups, one should turn the other cheek. Jesus and Paul did so under other circumstances—and in an absolute manner at the time of their martyrdom. In situations that are deteriorating, the enforcement of strict justice may become unrealistic, and the acceptance of suffering through love may be the only solution. Sometimes, however, for the very good of those who are attacked and of those who attack, we ought to defend the former (including ourselves) by word and action. At other times, for the good of the attackers and with the hope that they will reconsider, we ought to accept abuse, but without masochism or indignity.

Thus Ronald Rolheiser wisely gives this advice:

> When we absorb abuse, even with the highest religious motives, we do not take away the sin, we enable it. Jesus confronted dysfunction, even as he gave himself over in love. Sometimes the loving thing to do is not the gentle,

accommodating, and long-suffering one. In the face of positive abuse or clinical dysfunction, Christian discipleship can demand hard confrontation and perhaps even a distancing of ourselves from the person or persons who are causing the tension.[12]

Assessing such situations requires prayer in order that we not lose sight of the radicalness of the Gospel. We must have confidence that the Holy Spirit will instill the wisdom "so that you may discern what is the will of God—what is good and acceptable and perfect" (Rom 12:2) and the strength to put it into practice.

In the "Our Father," a petition says, "Forgive us our debts, as we also have forgiven our debtors" (Matt 6:12). And Jesus adds: "If you forgive others their trespasses, your heavenly Father will also forgive you; but if you do not forgive others, neither will your Father forgive your trespasses" (Matt 6:14–15). This passage seems to suggest that the pardon granted by God is conditioned by the pardon people grant to one another. And surely this impression raises questions.

Moreover, a parable recounted by Matthew seems to confirm the conditional character of divine pardon. After proclaiming the necessity of forgiving seventy times seven times, Jesus tells that terrible story in which an official to whom the king has remitted a large debt refuses to act in the same way toward a servant who owes him a small amount. Learning of this ungrateful and pitiless behavior, the angry king has the official arrested and handed over to the torturers until he pays his whole debt (Matt 18:21–35).

At first glance, this is a poor image of God: a being who goes back on his pardon and exercises justice with severity and cruelty. But to think so would be to miss the point of the parable. Rather, the emphasis is on the logic that carries the believer from God-given forgiveness to the forgiveness granted among human beings. Not only does divine pardon precede human pardon, but there is a huge disproportion between the debts remitted. Listening to the parable, we are urged to recognize the inconsistency of our behavior when, ignoring all that God has forgiven us, we refuse

---

12. Rolheiser, *Sacred Fire*, 163.

to forgive the little wrongs that others have done us. To admit this inconsequence is to open ourselves to conversion and salvation. That is what the parable is intended to effect in us.

But what is to be said about the conclusion of that parable? Its harshness is meant to produce in us a salutary fear, the fear that we might eschew forgiveness altogether because we (not God!) are harsh. Obviously, one need not interpret the parable to the letter. Educated Christians may hold, with Aquinas, that God does not change his mind, does not put people to torture, and does not refuse anyone his pardon. Problems with pardon do not arise on God's side, but on ours.

God wants to pardon and never withdraws his offer. But human beings can refuse this gift. They have been created free; they can say yes, and they can equally well say no. In refusing to forgive others, they say no to the divine offer of pardon by rendering themselves incapable of receiving it. Thus the two stages in the parable — the debtor-creditor's incoherence and God's angry response — are actually an indivisible whole. Because of the Incarnation, people who do not forgive the other members of Christ's Body put themselves into a psychological position where they cannot really accept the forgiveness of Christ. It is precisely this disastrous situation that is to be feared because it is psychologically and spiritually much worse than physical torture.

Thus, divine pardon precedes human repentance and love. Indicative of the standard contrary view, according to which repentance precedes pardon, is the quasi-unanimous misreading of an episode in Luke's Gospel, about "a woman in the city, who was a sinner" (7:37a), where Jesus said: "Her sins, which were many, have been forgiven; *hence* she has shown great love. But the one to whom little is forgiven, loves little" (v. 47; italics added). In this context, the Greek *oti* must be translated as "since" or as "hence" (as in the NRSV, which I have just quoted) and definitely not as "because," as in many other translations. The meaning is that she expressed her love *as a result of* having been forgiven, not that she was forgiven because she had loved *before* being forgiven.[13] The

---

13. Mary Magdalene is portrayed, along with three other forgiven

same response must apply to our love and forgiveness for others: since we are loved and forgiven by God, we must love and forgive our neighbor. Hence, St. Paul advises us, "As the Lord has forgiven you, so you also must forgive" (Col 3:13).

The parable and the "Our Father" unveil very high stakes. What can you do if you do not feel capable of pardoning another "from your heart" (Matt 18:35)? We must view the act of pardon within the context where grace and time do their work. If, under the shock of the blow received, we begin by rejecting the very prospect of forgiving, the parable of the two sons can encourage us. It reminds us that the one who first refused to obey his father later changed his mind and did what his father commanded (Matt 21:28–31). The Holy Spirit alone can grant us the capacity to forgive. That grace acts over the course of time and adapts itself to our limitations.

The crucial thing is to be willing to engage in a process of reconciliation. God asks no one to adopt an unsustainable rhythm. Hence the importance of taking one step at a time and of distinguishing different phases—not necessarily chronological—in a journey of forgiving whose length varies enormously depending on individual backgrounds.

The first phase is the decision not to take revenge. This resolution is all the more difficult to make when one is troubled by not having defended oneself adequately in the first place. To strike back and to score a few points might have the advantage of restoring a better self-image. But one must renounce both the pleasure of taking revenge and the illusion of strength that accompanies it.

A second phase consists in being fair to the person who is in the wrong. If our work or a particular situation requires objectively that one collaborate with or render a service to that person, one should do it, however difficult it may be.

---

sinners, namely King David, St. Peter, and the crucified "good thief," in Peter Paul Rubens's extraordinary painting, now kept in Munich's Alte Pinakothek, which I contemplated with admiration and emotion in 1978. I hope some of my readers have visited or will visit this great museum.

Another step to take is to talk to the person and clarify what happened. If this dialogue has some chance of success, one should risk it. As we have seen, Jesus recommends such action in a passage that precedes (and balances out) the one calling for forgiving seventy times seven times: "If another member of the church sins against you, go and point out the fault when the two of you are alone. If the member listens to you, you have regained that one" (Matt 18:15). What follows in the text suggests the possibility of involving other people. In the absence of the aggressors, pardon can be given in silence; at other times, it should form part of a process of confrontation. In the life of a married couple, for instance, only some combination of frank dialogue and forgiveness can ensure a fidelity that is maintained without damage to their psychological health.

Up to this point we have not discussed emotions. That is because forgiveness involves much more than emotions, namely acts, as we have just seen. We can enter into the process of pardoning long before we feel positive toward those who have hurt us. But feelings are nevertheless very influential, and the experience of indignation, revolt, powerlessness, hatred, antipathy, resentment, contempt, or the desire for retribution can be overwhelming. We must admit that we are unable to govern our emotions directly. They can be altered by new perceptions, by a change of outlook or atmosphere. It is enough to desire that negative feelings may pass. Nothing more is asked of us than to be open to the grace that gradually operates in us. Jesus alone cures our wounds—sometimes quickly, but generally slowly. "By his wounds you have been healed" (Isa 53:5, as quoted in 1 Pet 2:24).

Prayer is equally indispensable. We have to pray for ourselves, that we become capable of forgiving. We must also pray for those who have wronged, offended, or injured us, that they may learn to love. Thanks to prayer, painful events that have marked us will come to be placed in a Christian context and will thus be relativized. This context is well presented by St. Paul, when he writes that God has set reconciliation in motion in the world:

> So if anyone is in Christ, there is a new creation: everything old has passed away; see, everything has become new! All this is from God, who reconciled us to himself through Christ, and has given us the ministry of reconciliation; that is, in Christ God was reconciling the world to himself, not counting their trespasses against them, and entrusting the message of reconciliation to us. (2 Cor 5:17-19)

This chapter has offered an interpretation of radicalism that is not toned down. In closing, let us return to the key idea that the radicalism of the Gospel makes sense only in relation to the kingdom. The different forms of renunciation are subordinated to the presence of the Father in his incarnate Son, to the action of God renewing humanity through the life of Jesus. In a world where injustice so often prevails, only the cross is the answer to the problem of evil. It expresses God's response to the negative side of human history. But the cross exists for the sake of the resurrection: the negative is assumed by the positive, which encompasses it. Although the exact role of the negative escapes us to a considerable extent, faith allows us to counter it thanks to radical actions in our concrete circumstances.

The entire Bible conveys intense faith and unrestrained love of life. The Jewish "shalom" is based on the fact that God wills and brings about the good of his people. In the same way, it is out of gratefulness for the life given and given again by the Creator that the Maccabees accepted martyrdom (1 Macc 7). The positive appears also in the beatitudes, when Jesus declares "happy" those who suffer for the kingdom. The Wisdom of Solomon addresses God as "O Lord, you who love the living" (11:26). Comparing himself to the good shepherd who gives his life for his sheep, Jesus sums up the meaning of his mission in these words: "I came that they may have life, and have it abundantly" (John 10:10).

6

Toward a Synthesis

Having explored self-realization and the radical Gospel, we can tackle our central question: Are these ideals incompatible, or can they coexist, indeed fuse with one another? Evidently, we cannot ignore the fact that Christian radicalism rules out the way in which, *in fact*, self-realization is generally carried out. In light of the drastic prescriptions of the Sermon on the Mount and of the urgings of Jesus to deny oneself, take up one's cross, and give up one's life, it is clear that the Gospel demands a heroism at the opposite pole from current wisdom. Its message unmasks the superficiality of self-realization as it is ordinarily understood. The loftiness of Christianity, expressed in Jesus' command to "Be perfect, therefore, as your heavenly Father is perfect" (Matt 5:48), brings out by way of contrast the restricted horizon and the limitations of humanism.

To ensure that we are not going to outline a facile reconciliation between these two ideals, let us begin by listening to St. Paul.

> Let no one deceive you with empty words, for because of these things the wrath of God comes on those who are disobedient. Therefore do not be associated with them. For once you were darkness, but now in the Lord you are light. Live as children of light—for the fruit of the

light is found in all that is good and right and true. Try to find out what is pleasing to the Lord. Take no part in the unfruitful works of darkness, but instead expose them. (Eph 5:6-11)

Nevertheless, in the same Letter, St. Paul remarks, "He who loves his wife loves himself. For no one ever hates his own body, but he nourishes and tenderly cares for it, just as Christ does for the church" (Eph 5:28b-29).

Love of Self

Loving oneself is required if a person is to become self-transcendent. In this section, we briefly examine the thought of Aristotle, Augustine of Hippo, and Thomas Aquinas on love of self.

The philosopher Aristotle has rendered a great service to many students by distinguishing between three kinds of friendship. The first two have utility or pleasure as goals:

> Those who love each other for utility love the other not in his own right, but insofar as they gain some good for themselves from him. The same is true of those who love for pleasure; for they like a witty person not because of his character, but because he is pleasant to them.[1]

Aristotle characterizes the third and best type of friendship as follows:

> Complete friendship is the friendship of good people similar in virtue [*aretē*, better translated as "excellence"]; for they wish goods in the same way to each other insofar as they are good, and they are good in their own right. Now those who wish goods to their friend for the friend's own sake are friends most of all; for they have this attitude because of the friend himself. . . . It is reasonable that this sort of friendship is enduring, since it embraces in itself all the features that friends must have. For the

---

1. Aristotle, *Nicomachean Ethics*, book VIII, chap. 3, §2.

cause of every friendship is good or pleasure, either unqualified or for the lover. [2]

Aristotle believes that love for oneself is obtained among true friends. He even makes bold to declare that when one is a friend of someone else, one is at the same time a friend of oneself. He then loves himself, or, more precisely, "he wishes and does them [his actions] for his own sake, since he does them for the sake of his thinking part" (*tou gar dianoētikou*).[3] It is not his lower part, with its physical desires, that in the first place benefits, but his higher part, namely the part that understands what is good—in other words, the part that finds contentment in activities that are "beautiful" (*kalon*), according to the old Greek civic ideals.[4] So, for Aristotle, enlightened self-love consists in loving the higher part of one's soul.

By engaging in friendships that are enduring, wise people attain a state of happiness. Moreover, they do good works not only for a few friends but also for their city and even for the whole human race. However, as regards intimate friends, Aristotle tells us that the genuine friend is willing to sacrifice money, honor, all kinds of goods, and even his life for them.[5]

In *Teaching Christianity*, the theologian Augustine expounds what he thinks is the right order of love. He refers to Jesus' two commandments:

> "The first is, 'Hear, O Israel: the Lord our God, the Lord is one; you shall love the Lord your God with all your heart, and with all your soul, and with all your mind, and with all your strength.' The second is this, 'You shall love your neighbor as yourself.' There is no other commandment greater than these." (Mark 12:29–31)

---

2. Aristotle, *Nicomachean Ethics*, book VIII, chap. 3, §6–7.

3. Aristotle, *Nicomachean Ethics*, book IX, chap. 4, §3.

4. Aristotle, *Nicomachean Ethics*, book IX, chap. 8, §9.

5. Aristotle, *Nicomachean Ethics*, book VIII, chap. 1, §3–4, and book IX, chap. 8, §9–10.

Augustine comments:

> When indeed love of God is put first, and the manner of that love is clearly prescribed, indicating that everything else is to converge on it, nothing seems to be said about love of yourself. But when it says, "You shall love your neighbor as yourself," love of yourself by yourself is being simultaneously included.[6]

As a result, "the supreme reward is that we should enjoy him [God] and that all of us who enjoy him should also enjoy one another in him."[7]

Insofar as the philosopher-theologian Aquinas is concerned, in his *Summa contra Gentiles* he sees a *logical* priority of interest in oneself over interest in others:

> In fact, the love that a person has for others arises in him from the love that he has for himself, for a person stands in relation to a friend as he does to himself. But a person loves himself inasmuch as he wishes the good for himself, just as he loves another person by wishing him good. So, by the fact that a person is interested in his own good he is led to develop an interest in another person's good. Hence, because a person hopes for good from some other person, a way develops for him to love that other person in himself, from whom he hopes to attain the good. Indeed, a person is loved in himself when the lover wishes the good for him, even if the lover may receive nothing from him.[8]

In his Commentary of Aristotle's *Nicomachean Ethics*, Aquinas, like Aristotle, his favorite philosopher, situates his convictions about love of self in the context of friendship and rationality. First, he links together love of self and friendship:

> Everyone especially wishes good to himself. Evidently then a man ought to love himself most of all. . . . The reason is that all the attributes of friendship, which are

---

6. Augustine, *Teaching Christianity*, book 1, 26(27), 118.
7. Augustine, *Teaching Christianity*, book 1, 32(35), 122.
8. Aquinas, *Gentiles*, chap. 153; translation slightly modified.

considered in reference to others, are derived from the amicable relation a person bears towards himself. . . . Friendship consists in a kind of oneness that especially belongs to a man in relation to himself.⁹

And second, his argument ends with virtuous rationality:

> The more someone loves an object the more he loves what is more principal in it. . . . Therefore, he who loves his intellect or reason, and treats it well seems to be *philautos* or a lover of self most of all. . . . The intellect always chooses what is best for itself. . . . The virtuous person chooses the great good of virtue instead of all external goods; and so he loves himself most."¹⁰

In his *Summa Theologiae*, Aquinas contrasts love-of-friendship with love-of-concupiscence. Love-of-friendship consists in a union between two persons, with a mutual attention to, and promotion of, the goodness of the loved one. Love-of-concupiscence consists in desiring some particular good (e.g., wine, virtue, or some quality of a person) for the sake of someone else or for one's sake. Thus, I can desire something that will be a means to the other's well-being or to my own well-being. Most of the time, Thomas talks of love-of-concupiscence as desiring some good for the desiring individual's own sake, that is, as self-centered.

Furthermore, there is a complementarity between love-of-concupiscence and love-of-friendship. Aquinas does not extol the second at the expense of the first. For him there is no opposition between *eros* and *agapē*. Influenced by Dionysius, who wrote that the full meaning of *eros* incorporates the meaning of *agapē*, Thomas uses *amor* in a broad sense and ascribes a technical sense to *dilectio*.¹¹ His model is union and sharing. The virtue of prudence is called for, in order to adjudicate, according to the criteria of justice and charity, when the relevant value to be actualized in a

---

9. Aquinas, *Commentary*, lecture 8, nos. 1858–60.

10. Aquinas, *Commentary*, lecture 9, nos. 1868, 1869, 1877, and 1882.

11. In Aquinas's commentary on *The Divine Names*, *dilectio* renders *agape*; in *Summa Theologiae*, I–II, q. 26, a. 3, *dilectio* is associated with *electio* and thus takes on a philosophical meaning.

particular situation is the good-for-me or the good-for-the-other. As a matter of fact, these two can coincide. Aquinas observes that, although in self-gift many lower goods are often given up, self-love is never absent insofar as the highest good of the soul—charity—is not lost but increased.

On the other hand, even though love-of-concupiscence and love-of-friendship are structurally similar and are both indispensable, the latter is said to be higher than the former. For instance, in answering the question whether to be loved is more proper to charity than to love, Aquinas's negative answer starts with a quote not from the Bible but from the merely human wisdom of Aristotle, whom he calls "the Philosopher," a non-Christian thinker, to the effect that friendship results more in loving than in being loved.[12] Since the supernatural builds upon the natural, love-of-friendship is taken up in charity. The "more . . . than" indicates an emphasis on loving, and yet not the exclusion of being loved.

Aquinas explains:

> In love-of-concupiscence, the lover is carried out of himself in the sense that he is not content to enjoy what is already in his possession, but is anxious to enjoy something which is as yet outside his grasp; but since he is anxious to have that external good for himself, he is not carried out of himself *tout court*; the ultimate term of his feeling lies within himself. In love-of-friendship, however, the ultimate term of the person's feeling is located outside of him *tout court*, for he wants some good thing for his friend, and works for it, by caring and providing for him, for his friend's sake.[13]

To sum up this section: On love of self, Aristotle offers philosophical considerations; Augustine finds theological support in Jesus' teaching; and Aquinas submits a view that is both philosophical and theological. Still, whatever their differences, all three are agreed that there is no complete love without love of oneself.

---

12. Aquinas, *Summa Theologiae*, II–II, q. 27, a. 1.
13. Aquinas, *Summa Theologiae*, I–II, q. 28, a. 3.

From the Ego to the Self

We have noted that in modern times, the West has emphasized the intrinsic worth of the individual. This is a sound achievement since it has fostered respect for the rights of the person. But an insistence on individual importance can too easily slide into the cult of the ego. When that happens, the ego becomes an absolute, evaluating everything in relation to itself. Then the "ego trip" that characterizes adolescence is prolonged indefinitely into a pseudo-adulthood.

If egoism constitutes a deformation of a moral kind, which hurts other people, the psychological egocentrism of which we are speaking is also at fault and requires an explanation. This egotism betrays an anxiety concerning oneself. It is a preoccupation that derives from the fact that a fundamental desire has yet to be satisfied: the desire for proof that the author of the world and of life cares deeply about me and loves me passionately, despite all my mistakes and imperfections.[14]

Christianity does not consider the ego an illusion. It recognizes the need to be valued as a demand set in the human heart by the Creator. All people want to prove themselves. Think of the immense satisfaction babies feel when they first grasp things and manipulate their physical environment. Throughout and beyond one's accomplishments, each person wishes (and legitimately so) to be seen as special, unique, and irreplaceable. Lasting peace derives from the knowledge that one is not only loved, but also lovable.

While taking up all that psychology and ethics have to say about the increase of self-esteem, Christianity grants much more. The value of a person is based on the fact that God has created her and offered her two great gifts: freedom in Jesus Christ and a share in the trinitarian life. Just because it is founded on the love of God, self-esteem is not restricted to being an extrinsic characteristic. The love of God, in fact, allows a person to internalize this esteem and make it her own.

Experience demonstrates, however, that every truly religious person cannot be content to live within the limits of the individual

---

14. See Roy, *Embracing Desire*, 68–72.

self. If we reflect seriously on self-realization, we have to ask what "self" we are talking about. Maturity consists in shedding the illusion of a purely individual ego so as to rejoice that one is integrated into a greater whole. For the Christian tradition, what is illusory is not the ego, but the isolated ego, namely the ego that fails to understand that the experience of belonging is constitutive of the self.

It is here that the distinction between the ego and the self proves useful.[15] The ego is the aspect of a person that feels, protects, and promotes one's individual identity. The self is the aspect that wants to participate in an ensemble greater than itself. When a person is persuaded of being placed on this earth to live out, in suffering and joy, a profound mystery of love, he ceases to be obsessed by the "me" and has already begun to explore the religious universe. He also escapes the trap of construing the passage from ego to self as a self-enlargement that is in fact mere ego-aggrandizement. Unfortunately, one can enjoy the illusion of becoming a fuller self without being actually committed to other people and consequently without really participating in a broader self.

Each one of us is essentially relational; we do not realize ourselves except in contact with others. As Teilhard de Chardin affirms, true union increases one's personal identity. He wrote, "*union differentiates.*"[16] But there is more. Through knowledge and love, we can in a certain sense dwell in one another. One day, a woman who had just lost her son said to me, "For us parents, our children are ourselves." At the level of the family as at the level of all humanity, there is a feeling of solidarity and communion, which makes each self more than itself. Having the same origin and the same end, we all participate in the same divine reality. This profound insight renders possible a religious detachment, a certain distancing from what we have become, and a decision to abandon

---

15. The importance of the distinction between ego and self was brought home to me by Sebastian Moore's writings. See Roy, "Human Desire," 53–66. See also Roy, *Mystical Consciousness*, 115–43.

16. de Chardin, *Phenomenon*, 262; italics his.

oneself to the goodness of life. It empowers us to persevere in self-transcendence and to open ourselves to the whole of reality.[17]

While becoming fully oneself, each person can make a contribution to the world, according to the design of God, which embraces all people. For each of us is more than just one ego; we are what God wants to make of us by locating us in history as irreplaceable agents. Even if some apparently refuse to join in the common movement, that does not prevent God, the master of events, from bringing about a better humanity through the meanders of their long march.[18]

The Horizon of an Unsuspected Reality

Christian revelation unveils a reality much more vast and sublime than the one envisioned by materialism and even greater than the one glimpsed by people who are concerned with the best of secular values. That reality, which the New Testament calls the kingdom of God, is equivalent to the final coming together of the human race into the mystery that calls them forward. This reality includes the dimension of the future, of hope, and of the promises of God.

According to Emil Fackenheim, this meaning of "reality" contradicts a frequent understanding of "self-realization."

> Religion also is interpreted in terms of self-realization. The fact that many modern definitions of religion do not even include God indicates what has happened: religion has been transformed from a total integration of life through relation to a supernatural God into total integration through self-realization. The convictions leading to this transformation are again the same: all meaning that the individual can find in his life is inherent in his own nature; and any meaning that he cannot find in himself is both unattainable and practically irrelevant, therefore properly to be ignored.[19]

---

17. This profound insight is illustrated at length in Francis, *Fratelli Tutti*.
18. Roy, *Engaging*, 226–34.
19. Fackenheim, *Quest*, essay entitled "Self-Realization and the Search for

For Jews and Christians, the coming of God is part of reality. The presence and action of God in time relativize the current moment. On the one hand, they situate it within a long-range movement; on the other hand, they allow us to better enjoy this limited present, a stage on the way to the promised salvation.

Another metaphor, that of the Body of Christ (1 Cor 12:12–31), also illustrates this reality. Each Christian is part of the Body and concerned about the whole. The interests, values, and goals that polarize the energies of the individual are integrated into the great project—the growth of the Body of Jesus Christ. One finds joy, then, in mothering and fathering human beings. "When a woman is in labor, she has pain, because her hour has come. But when her child is born, she no longer remembers the anguish because of the joy of having brought a human being into the world" (John 16:21).

This joy can also be found in caring for the sick and the weak. Just as, in view of the good of the whole, the healthy members of a body give much attention and care to ill or infirm members, a oneness of destiny leads us to extend to widening circles the kind of care a mother or father spontaneously shows to a child in need.

The reality that Christianity recognizes includes the fact of evil. When self-realization has no religious horizon, most of the time it is incapable of dealing with such misfortunes as major disappointments, failures, defeats, humiliations, blows, betrayals, permanent psychic wounds, moral weaknesses, prolonged illness—in short, excessive sufferings that surpass anything that one might possibly gain from them on the human level.

By contrast, far from denying evil, the Gospel confronts it directly and offers a practical solution: the cross. Jesus' and the believers' praxis defeats evil by inspiring acts of generosity, non-defensiveness, and hope, which surpass ordinary wisdom. Those who open themselves to reconciliation absorb hatred in their bodies and bring peace (Eph 2:14–17). What St. Paul calls "God's foolishness" proves to be "God's wisdom" (1 Cor 1:18—2:16). In action as in suffering, the cross sums up and subsumes all that is

---

God: A Critique of Modern Humanism and a Defence of Jewish Supernaturalism," 27–51, at 28.

negative in human existence. In overcoming evil by good, inertia by initiative, and egoism by self-giving, the cross becomes the unique solution to the problem of evil. It is as much the law of life as the law of Christ. Because of the resurrection, it has an eschatological value. It is the cross that operates now and will triumph at the end of time.

This vision of faith constitutes the horizon which throws light upon everything else. Whenever standard wisdom loses sight of Jesus' example, of the Father's immense love, and of the Holy Spirit's influence upon our collective destiny, the radical Gospel becomes a scandal. It is the very mystery of God, in fact, that is offered to us. A single mystery of love, self-transcendence, and fullness can be seen in the Trinity as well as in the creative and liberating action of God in which we play a part. Through earthly mediations, and following the lead of Jesus, it is possible for us to leave behind, one by one, various stages of ego-development in order to be taken up into the divine self.

Self-Gift

It is in this perspective that we can understand the possibility of making a total gift of ourselves. This gift of self goes beyond simple renunciation, which arises from the necessity of making choices. The normal exercise of human freedom implies that an individual chooses a certain good and therefore must set aside another, since she cannot experience everything simultaneously. She cannot concentrate on some good work, for instance, without renouncing other equally worthwhile commitments. Renunciation also relates to her scale of preferences and hierarchy of values. When she gives precedence to a higher good, the pleasure that might have been derived from a lower one is forsaken. This latter form of renunciation can be very demanding. For example, those who are deeply immersed in the Gospel must be ready to sacrifice many lesser goods, in order that the Good News may be brought to the poor and divine love may be recognized by as many as possible.

SELF-ACTUALIZATION AND THE RADICAL GOSPEL

Even in contexts that are not explicitly religious, people discover in themselves, often with surprise, riches that relativize their daily concerns. They become convinced that generosity does not impoverish. Speaking to Romeo, Juliet exclaims,

> My bounty is as boundless as the sea,
> My love as deep; the more I give to thee
> The more I have, for both are infinite.[20]

Aside from certain forms of spontaneous heroism (for example, the mother who throws herself upon her child's attacker, or the lifeguard who rushes to the rescue of an imprudent swimmer pulled into strong sea undertows), human beings cannot consistently endanger their life without reference to an ultimate value, although such a reference may remain unarticulated. How can they sacrifice themselves for an equal if a common destiny does not unite them in an adventure that is greater than them all? It was *to God* that Jesus offered his life at the moment of death: "Father, into your hands I commend my spirit" (Luke 23:46).

Whether we call it the kingdom of God, the Body of Christ, the Vine that Jesus is, with us as its branches, the Holy City, or the New Jerusalem, Christianity presents a dynamic and transcendent reality that attracts and surrounds us. At the heart of this reality is the example of Jesus—his way of life, death, and resurrection. We can resolve to transcend ourselves in favor of justice and other human values to the extent that we believe these efforts will not be in vain.

Faith in the resurrection qualifies the natural pursuit of self-fulfillment. Through the experience of making choices dictated by the highest values of the hierarchy, one becomes aware that the ego does not have to be realized in all its aspects. As Matthew 5:29–30 indicates metaphorically, it is better to accept being deprived of an eye or a hand than to go unmaimed into perdition. This explains Christ's saying that "Those who lose their life for my sake, and for the sake of the gospel, will save it" (Mark 8:35). To lose one's life means to lose a part of one's *ego*, or (in some cases) all of it. But in

---

20. William Shakespeare, *Romeo and Juliet*, Act 2, Scene 2, lines 133–35.

losing one's life for Christ's sake, one's *self* or one's deepest being is saved, as it is united with God and with all those who belong to the Body of Christ. As St. Irenaeus put it, "The glory of God is the living person (*vivens homo*) and the life of such a person is the vision of God."[21]

A purely human motivation of an ethical nature cannot lead a person as far in the gift of self as a religious motivation. The latter is based on discovering God in Jesus:

> Hope does not disappoint us, because God's love has been poured into our hearts through the Holy Spirit that has been given to us. For while we were still weak, at the right time Christ died for the ungodly. Indeed, rarely will anyone die for a righteous person—though perhaps for a good person someone might actually dare to die. (Rom 5:5–8)

The experience of having been loved so intensely results in a longing to help others make the same discovery. Having known a God who gives us and wants back the best of our selves, we wish that others will become their best selves. Because we know the signs of hunger for love, we recognize them in the eyes of human beings we meet. "When he saw the crowds, he had compassion for them, because they were harassed and helpless, like sheep without a shepherd" (Matt 9:36).

Thus, we grow in sensitivity and compassion. Our "charity" (*agapē*) can become what St. Paul describes in the thirteenth chapter of his first letter to the Corinthians. It does not always have to be emotionally felt in order to be genuine and effective. Whatever the atmosphere surrounding a person, if she is loving, she will not be stinting in her efforts; she will be generous and self-transcending, because she knows that God is thinking of her. Dazzled by God, she seeks to share with others what she has found to be the best part of life—this God of love. And if she becomes demanding of others, it is because she is persuaded that they, too, ought to grow

---

21. Irenaeus, *Against Heresies*, book 4, chap. 20, no. 7.

in love. She recalls the word of Jesus: "It is more blessed to give than to receive" (Acts 20:35).[22]

The Fascination for God

What exactly is the depth of the self that the cross and the resurrection allow to be saved? It is the most fundamental aspect of human relationships. It is realized by entering into a communion with the Father, the Son, and the Holy Spirit. In realizing it, one finds a priceless treasure worthy of having everything else subordinated to it. "For where your treasure is, there your heart will be also" (Matt 6:21; see 13:44).

Such a centering on God revolutionizes the existence of those who believe in him. Communion with God is the keystone of the Christian temple. Only friendship with God can begin to satisfy the human person. Such a relationship explains why the divine Law goes beyond the capacities of human morality. "You shall be holy, for I the Lord your God am holy" (Lev 19:2). This demanding imitation calls for costly sacrifices on the part of believers. Their personalities, marked by sin and the disequilibrium that results from it, cannot be easily integrated into the primacy of the divine. A tension arises between the fascination exercised by this spellbinding God and the limited desires of our daily life.

And yet this fascination must be developed. Unfortunately, many Christians have no real interest in God. They think of God only to thank him for creation and to receive moral help from him. This stance brings about an ethical conversion but not a genuine religious conversion. Thus, Christ becomes for them the example and guarantor of what they want to accomplish. Jesus appears as the man who loves life and supports what is human. In that way he reveals something of the Father. But his invitation to become involved with God is not necessarily welcomed by these believers.

Does the absence of interest in God deprive believers of something important? Does it prevent them from struggling

---

22. On the issue of self-gift, see Roy, *Embracing Desire*, 42–48.

against their own defects and attaining self-fulfillment? Must one love God with one's whole heart in order to be able to love others in that way? The answer to these questions cannot but be affirmative because the values that one recognizes as preeminent become idols—values as noble as one's own personal growth and that of others, or the struggle for more justice and less misery—insofar as the living God does not hold first place in one's life. Fortunately, it happens that God makes himself present in the depths of the human heart even if many people cannot give a name to the fascinating mystery that touches them. But lacking religious detachment in the pursuit of their goals, many feel in themselves a certain rigidity, which can vitiate their search for these values.

Those who experience the attraction of the infinite Mystery are convinced that God alone is the ultimate good for each person and for the whole human race. Self-realization and success in life stop being great preoccupations. The ethical commitment remains serious and in fact increases. But self-realization comes to be perceived as already given and assured. That is why one ceases to be excessively concerned with signs of success and becomes more interested in God. From this attitude there arises a definite joy, a harmony in the daily comings and goings, and also great freedom. Interest in God crowns the opening to all of reality. Profound gratitude develops in the person to whom God has manifested his presence.

In this climate of grace, interest in God and Gospel radicalism resolutely interact. Speaking of "costly grace," Dietrich Bonhoeffer emphasizes both the courage demanded of Christ's disciples and the fact that this courage is given by God. This gift of God is more fundamental than the human response, although the two prove to be inseparable. A reversal of perspective becomes operative as soon as one becomes more attentive to grace than to human effort. In fact, self-transcendence and self-realization are both given by the Holy Spirit.[23]

From this awareness arises an atmosphere of hope and humility, personal peace, and dedication to the work of our vocation.

23. Bonhoeffer, *The Cost*, 35–47.

There is therefore no need to be overanxious about our limited attainment of self-transcendence and self-realization. Of course, we must seek ways to foster such attainment. But the best means is by concerning ourselves first with the Father, the source of love; with Jesus, who is our companion; with the Holy Spirit, who inspires us and assumes the responsibility for making a success of our life; and with those around us, including their values, their needs, and their objective appeals directed toward us.

Happiness and Finitude

To experience this interest in God with full authenticity, one must renounce happiness. "Happiness" here refers to the kind of security and plenitude enjoyed in the mother's womb before birth. As soon as we are born, we enter into a process in which we must deal with expectations and frustrations. To accept the limits of reality proves difficult emotionally. That is why we remain nostalgic for the uncomplicated state symbolized by the mother's womb or by a romanticized image of childhood. In adolescents and immature adults, the pursuit of this unattainable goal sometimes becomes intense. Nothing is more disappointing and destructive, for example, than a love experience based on the search for that kind of happiness. The more one wants it, the less one will find it.

This happiness in the strict sense, which we should renounce, differs from happiness in the broad sense. The latter, in fact, is equivalent to the pleasure, satisfaction, joy, or peace that accompanies activities that are interesting, meaningful, and brought to fruition. In the measure in which people take a genuine interest in their surroundings and engage in meaningful activities, they have this positive experience. It would be foolish to deprive oneself of this happiness since religious maturity entails it. In contrast to the illusory happiness that certain adults childishly pursue, the happiness we are talking about has nothing exalted about it. And yet, how rewarding it is! When we welcome the personal presence of God and of the kingdom in which he gathers all those who try to love, we cannot but taste that incomparable peace, "not . . . as the world gives" (John 14:27), and that lasting joy of which Jesus says, "no one will take your joy from you" (John 16:22).

But why should we renounce happiness understood in the strict sense? It is because this happiness can only take the form of an idol, that is to say, a limited reality of which we ask a vaguely infinite good. And behind all the idols in which we could place our hope, we find the principal idol, the ego. Is it not the ego that we deify when engaging in activities from which we expect total happiness? Still, we know that neither the ego nor anything in this world is infinite. The ego cannot therefore satisfy itself and it cannot be satisfied by anything finite. In this respect, the myth of unlimited potential, which certain psychologists invite us to actualize, proves deceptive; it usually sponsors changes in our relationships, lifestyle, or career that promise too much and thus inevitably end up in disappointment. Moreover, each time we absolutize the ego, we run the risk of hurting others, since we lose the freedom that allows unconditional respect for them, and we thereby diminish their freedom instead of reinforcing it. Idolatry, in fact, renders impossible the detachment and courage that are required to love wholeheartedly.

Commenting on "the twentieth-century demotic individual," which means "of the people" or, in other words, "the common man," Jacques Barzun describes his plight as "the longing for the limitless":

> His overriding taste was for the unconditioned Life. . . . For the large groups that until the mid-century had been disregarded and mistreated as inferiors, acquiring the common privileges and an increasing measure of respect naturally stimulated the desire for more. But the unconditioned life was something different from enjoying rights and decent treatment from one's fellows. It was to act as if nothing stood in the way of every wish. Such an attitude expects no rebuffs and overlooks those it provokes.[24]

---

24. Barzun, *From Dawn*, 781.

Gospel radicalism becomes possible when we give up the childish notion of happiness as fulfilling "the longing for the limitless." We then accept frustrations and suffering, make choices, and realize limited goals. We pursue significant values in a realistic fashion, taking successes and failures in stride. We accept our finiteness.

Renouncing happiness does not imply giving up one's love of life. If the Christian mystic lays aside his childish aspirations and abandons the search for a lost paradise, it is not in order to become a stoic. Far from resigning himself to what finite reality offers, he has discovered, on the contrary, a much broader and higher reality. The true adult turns his back on a paradise of the past and goes forward toward the one that lies ahead. What is the difference between these two attitudes? The search for a past paradise consists in trying to transform the finite into the infinite. Openness to the future paradise consists in accepting totally the finitude of our earthly life, viewing it against the horizon of the infinite. Without denying finitude, we welcome a gift of God that comes to us precisely through the finite. The very life of God is given to human beings through Jesus, who experienced finitude:

> Though he was in the form of God, he did not regard equality with God as something to be exploited, but emptied himself, taking the form of a slave, being born in human likeness. And being found in human form, he humbled himself and became obedient to the point of death—even death on a cross. Therefore God also highly exalted him and gave him the name that is above every name, so that at the name of Jesus every knee should bend, in heaven and on earth and under the earth, and every tongue should confess that Jesus Christ is Lord, to the glory of God the Father. (Phil 2:6–11)

The perplexing collision between the ideal of the Gospel and current wisdom is illuminating. It is through contact with what is great and beautiful that human reflection becomes aware of its deviations and begins to listen to its profound aspirations. Thus, in our chapter 2, the light of Christian revelation has helped us to uncover what is lacking in the tendency toward self-contentment. We then made an argument in favor of what Rousseau called "love of self," or love for oneself, in contrast to his (justified) negative view of "self-love."

Given the demands of the New Testament, some people infer that they must abandon the concern for self-fulfillment altogether. In chapter 1, we exposed the illusions that this stance often carries. Christians are entitled to trust that along with the assistance of grace, God calls them to develop all that is positive in human nature. And yet we must add that self-actualization, when pursued with religious faith, has an altered meaning that is much more profound than the purely secular one. Self-actualization is integrated into a much richer context—God's dream for humanity.

7

Rhythms and Readjustments

How can we take seriously the radicalism of the Gospel while being also concerned with our own personal development? This question raises problems about implementation. Let us therefore examine and discuss the rhythms, stages, and elements that contribute to advancement.

Complementary Rhythms

Living beings function according to rhythms. It is unhealthy to want to act always with maximum intensity or to seek continuous comfort. The book of Ecclesiastes wisely emphasizes the usefulness of respecting the alternating rhythms of major human experiences. Qoheleth (Ecclesiastes) states:

> For everything there is a season, and a time for every matter under heaven: a time to be born, and a time to die; . . . a time to weep, and a time to laugh; . . . a time to seek, and a time to lose; a time to keep, and a time to throw away; . . . a time to love, and a time to hate; a time for war, and a time for peace. (Eccl 3:1–8)

Let us recall what was said in chapter 3. When the radical Gospel directs human intentionality toward a supreme reality, the principle of limitation, which is the psyche, must balance out this forward movement with periods of rest and recuperation. Otherwise, the Christian ideal would become infected with megalomania or other mental illnesses. As a matter of fact, the saints tempered their austerities with activities that brought them a good deal of satisfaction. Unfortunately, hagiography has rarely noted this aspect of their wisdom. Unlike materialists, however, the saints did not suffer from an excess of leisure. They both transcended and realized themselves by concentrating on the highest values.

Still in chapter 3, we considered Maslow's principle that we should not be dependent on categories of exclusion when we think of the relationships between personal needs and interest in the outside world. Instead, his principle favors thinking according to a hierarchical integration. We must now draw the practical conclusion and envision life as alternating between complementary rhythms. These rhythms are many: prayer/commitment, solitude/solidarity, giving/receiving, being with/being for, leisure/work, and so forth.

In this regard, nothing is more treacherous than half-truths, namely pseudo-universal principles that transform into absolutes what cannot actually be more than partial aims.[1] Here are some examples: "Self-transcendence supposes that you have first achieved self-actualization. You have to think of yourself first. You cannot be at ease with other people unless you begin by feeling good about yourself. Be independent, be yourself, and do what feels good. If that offends others, too bad for them." Such erroneous maxims support the one-sided quest for self-fulfillment.

Here are a few more maxims, this time on the side of self-transcendence: "There is no use in forcing yourself into self-actualization; it is better not to cultivate it, but to take everything simply and to get interested in what lies around you, without introspection. Avoid being subjective; only pay attention to the objective needs of others. The group is more important than the individual. Only take care to love and give constantly—that

1. See Roy, *Feeling*, 82–96.

is the key to happiness. Trust people and they will become honest and generous."

The common defect in all these maxims is that they are excessive in their generality, which makes them exercise an impoverishing effect on those who attempt to apply them. Although many psychologists and preachers serve up such naïve pronouncements, experience teaches us that matters are not so simple. Several of these mottos are based on a false temporal or ontological priority: *first* this or that. Thus, they claim that individualism must come *before* altruism, or vice versa; or that subjectivity ought to be placed *over* objectivity, or vice versa. Such banalities consider only one side of the coin.

In contrast to this one-sidedness, the wise Jesus recognizes the healthy tension that must exist between two complementary attitudes: "Be wise as serpents and innocent as doves" (Matt 10:16). He not only says, "Peace I leave with you; my peace I give to you" (John 14:27), but also "Do not think that I have come to bring peace to the earth; I have not come to bring peace, but a sword" (Matt 10:34).

Alternation is not a mere compromise between the pursuit of happiness and self-abnegation. Instead, one thinks of oneself in order to be able to think of others. To take time for oneself, to rest and relax, to renew one's motivation and energies, to introduce some changes—all that can foster joyful, inventive, and well-adjusted commitment. Can one love another, with real interest in the other, and at the same time have in view one's self-realization? Purists would say no. And yet these two intentions can be united in a movement of coming and going, where one's attention is directed by turns toward the self and toward the other. If there is a problem, it is that people do not naturally love others right away. They must come to a standstill, reflect, pray, and open themselves to the grace of God in order to learn how to love and act harmoniously.

Far from suppressing the hierarchy of values, the law of alternation allows one to interpret the hierarchy dynamically. Any concrete application requires discernment. A superior value generally (though not always) takes precedence over a lesser value. For example, although pastoral work is obviously nobler than leisure, those who are engaged in the ministry must take time off for relaxation at regular intervals, even if important work is waiting to be done. Thus, when Jesus saw the disciples returning from their preaching, he said to them, "Come away to a deserted place all by yourselves and rest a while" (Mark 6:31). On the other hand, when an emergency arises, good pastors spontaneously realize that their leisure must be sacrificed.

Part of discernment consists in taking note of what suits various people and circumstances. The Gospel commands that either directly or indirectly we should make common cause with the poor, the underserved, and the despised. This supposes a disinterested love, since we are unlikely to get back as much as we give, although sometimes we do. But this commitment needs to be supported by reciprocal love, either in the same environment (when we receive some gratitude) or with different people in another setting.

In the same way, courageous parents can show self-sacrificial love toward a disabled child born to them, or to an emotionally abused child they have adopted. Or again, a married individual can decide to remain with an unfaithful or very difficult partner. Others devote themselves as psychiatrists, psychologists, or nurses, taking care of psychotics and neurotics, or the sick, the infirm, or the dying. All these forms of radicalism can be sustained only by periods of rest or leisure, during which strength is restored.

Readjustments and Reorientations

In addition to the alternations of complementary rhythms, life causes us to pass through various phases, during which we need to find new bearings. It then becomes imperative to adjust our ideas, reactions, attitudes, or ways of acting and to redirect our commitments and priorities, sometimes even to the extent of reinterpreting our ultimate goals. These periods of adjustment can prove very difficult. Having inherited from their grandparents a wisdom fashioned in the stable circumstances of an agricultural world, many people have not yet found the wisdom to live without too much disturbance amid the changes taking place with increasing frequency in the present world.

Traditionally, the criteria of goodness were by and large extrinsic. Most of the time, individual action was evaluated according to the yardstick of a group's principles, moral laws, and customs. In the twentieth century, however, the immense scope of contradictory ideas passed down by education and the mass media has caused the pendulum to swing to the other extreme, to subjectivism. The sphere of action has become psychologized, in the sense that it has become almost entirely subject to pre-moral considerations, as was explained in chapter 2.

In order to face up to the challenges presented by the various ages and stages of life and to handle the crises caused by inescapable circumstances, an individual must develop the ability to change. That supposes that he has a vision that places mobility ahead of immobility. It is not comfortable to practice fidelity through continual readjustment. It is often easier to transcend ourselves in a setting we have chosen than to become aware of what lies deeply buried in us, to bring to consciousness ambiguous and unsettling material, and thus to allow new possibilities of self-transcendence to emerge.

It is important to pay attention to the symptoms indicating that such a review is necessary. Someone may feel weary, dissatisfied, less and less motivated, anxious, vaguely guilty, or depressed without any particular reason—in short, she has ceased to function as she used to, and she no longer understands herself. Dwelling on these symptoms will normally lessen her commitment. And yet, if radicalism implies forward movement, she must state frankly that it is Gospel-like to recognize that she is in a questioning period and then seek out help toward a clearer understanding of her position.

What is radical, then, is to accept oneself with one's ambiguities. To be a pilgrim is to enter resolutely into the crisis, with the courage to face uncertainty and risk, and to confront doubts, regrets, fears, and complex problems. It is noble to arrive at the truth regarding one's real feelings, to unmask negative tendencies, to become more familiar with one's fantasies, desires, sexuality, and mode of relating to others—in sum, to accept all such psychic experiences and to integrate them into one's consciousness.

Some people feel guilty if they give up certain outlooks and options that have always been linked to a religious ideal. Other people are disturbed to discover their need to abandon viewpoints or preferences that were based on a superficial understanding of self-realization. When self-transcendence and self-actualization are misunderstood, it is hard to admit that our former way of seeing and choosing is no longer suited to what we have become or are called to become. Let us think of the Pharisee Paul, who had to renounce his legalistic past: "Forgetting what lies behind and straining forward to what lies ahead, I press on towards the goal" (Phil 3:13-14).

The danger to be avoided here is the cultivation of childishness in oneself or in others in the name of the Gospel. Passages in the New Testament dealing with radical demands can appear to be invitations to a false self-denial for people who are weak or in crisis. What belongs to a supra-moral context may serve to support action of an infra-moral kind. In this case, far from promoting personal growth, the religious ideal only contributes to the psychological stagnation of the individual who clings to a false notion of this ideal. Unfortunately, as we noted in chapter 1, the great Christian values can encourage attitudes of ill-considered devotion, submission to others, and self-annihilation before God.

Various phenomena then take place. A long period of frustration often induces fascination with the things we have always secretly desired. In the handling of possessions, leisure, or sexuality, we may become obsessed by the images of objects, pleasures, or experiences that we have been denied. Regrets concerning what we missed in the past may lead to the kind of lust for experiences that was described in chapter 2.

It can be the same with self-actualization: if it is too long neglected, it may suddenly be perceived as a sacred right, a matter of urgency, which is then striven after in an unsuitable way. In this case, the compulsion toward self-indulgence reduces other people to mere objects that must be grasped and enjoyed.

Moreover, apart from this type of fascination and obsession, one can also experience the phenomenon of "indigestion," wherein one vomits whatever was excessive, imposed, or badly understood in the restrictive practices of the past. Additionally, there may be a—hopefully temporary—backsliding when one's ethical system disintegrates.

We must not telescope this disturbing phase of human development. It would be artificial and unhealthy to stifle the appeals of the unconscious, to silence questions, and to continue as before, trying to maintain a spurious ideal of self-transcendence. During this phase, in fact, the gift of self is practically impossible, because the self that is to be given has been so weakened that it is virtually void. This is not the time to pose any challenge other than facing one's problems. Instead, the time has come to examine oneself, heal one's wounds, and renew oneself.

The same wisdom is required when a system of egotistical principles crumbles. One should not immediately and rigorously put forward the contrary ideal of self-transcendence. Again, the individual in this case has no true self to give. If he prematurely embraces the idea of self-giving, he will try to carry it out with the same clumsiness that characterized his search for individual happiness. He will easily become intoxicated by the illusion of his recent generosity. While applauding his efforts to take into consideration the good of others, it is necessary to allow him no longer to concentrate on performance but to open himself to a much-needed personal transformation, which is a matter more of grace than of striving.

The Role of Counseling or Therapy

Counseling or therapy can help enormously, provided that the counselor respects the moral and religious dimensions of the client. A psychological readjustment, if well done, can lead to reorientations of the moral and religious order. In the same way, spiritual direction allows links to be established between the psycho-moral modifications that are taking place and the Christian meaning of one's journey. The presence of a good listener helps the person to interiorize the fact that God sees with love and compassion all that the human being has within herself. Hope on the part of the therapist or spiritual guide plays a very significant role. It is not easy to let go of abnormalities in the line of either self-transcendence or self-actualization. To admit that one has attributed a false worth to oneself is risky; it can diminish her self-esteem and can cause discouragement and sometimes despair. It is important, therefore, that the discovery of negative aspects coincides with a discovery of positive aspects. The listener should help the person to find beauty in herself.

Regarding depression, many observers have noted a resemblance between depression and the way John of the Cross characterizes the second night of his mystical journey, namely the dark night of the spirit. For instance, in both situations the profound malaise that is felt often comes from a severe disappointment, which itself has its roots in a deep-set attachment to some person or some goal; the frustration that is experienced knocks off balance a person's desiring capacity.[2]

It is nonetheless very helpful to distinguish—without separating—the dark night and depression: the former is a *religious* phenomenon, in which people are worried about their relationship with God, whereas the latter is a *psychic* phenomenon, which John of the Cross calls *melancolía* and in which self-centered people are worried about their own situation.[3] In the dark night, one's desire to please God remains, even as one thinks he or she is not pleasing God; in depression, it is one's ability to desire that is impaired. Accordingly, the dark night is potentially liberating, whereas depression is usually debilitating.

However, both may coexist and constitute a single painful experience. Indeed, they have in common a feeling of meaninglessness, of having lost one's certitudes, of having hit an impasse

---

2. See Kristeva, *Black Sun*.

3. On *melancolía*, see John of the Cross, *Collected Works*, "The Ascent of Mount Carmel," Prologue 4.6 and II.13.6; "The Dark Night," I.4.3 and I.9.3.

from which there is no escape, and hence a sense of failure and of powerlessness. Thus, the psychiatrist Gerald May writes:

> My experience is that people often experience depression and the dark night at the same time. To say the least, the dark night can be depressing. Even if most of the experience feels liberating, it still involves loss, and loss involves grief, and grief may at least temporarily become depression. Conversely, a primary clinical depression can become part of a dark-night experience, just as any other illness can.[4]

Nevertheless, May cautions, "With today's understanding of the causes and treatment of depression, it makes more sense simply to identify depression where it exists and to treat it appropriately, regardless of whether it is associated with a dark-night experience."[5] We also ought to heed the remark by an excellent educator that "Conditions like clinical depression often have a genetic basis that no amount of religion can fix."[6] Therefore, we must avoid spiritualizing depression and vainly trying to fix it only with religious means.

Let me continue to contrast the two phenomena. On the one hand, the dark night of the spirit includes an impression of grave infidelity to Christ, of being wholly undeserving of divine mercy, of being ignored or abandoned by God. As we can no longer pray in an appropriate, "successful" manner, the communication with God seems to have broken down. Such a trial is an opportunity to become Christlike by letting the Holy Spirit purify our desires and rid us of attachments so as to be bound to the Father and to love our neighbors in a way that is freer and more mature because it has become fairly independent of what we get from God and from others.[7]

On the other hand, depression entails an excessive and unwarranted sense of guilt, a paralysis of the will, and the inability to

---

4. May, *Dark Night*, 156. See also May, *Care of Mind*, 84–92.
5. May, *Dark Night*, 157.
6. Manning, *Converting*, 5.
7. See FitzGerald, "Impasse," 410–35.

accomplish one's daily work or to engage in meaningful relationships or activities. As Zagano and Gillespie report,

> Diagnosis of depression requires five or more of the following symptoms, including a depressed mood and a loss of interest or pleasure present within a two-week period: 1) constant depressed mood; 2) lack of enjoyment or pleasure in most activities; 3) unaccounted for weight loss; 4) sleeplessness or over sleeping; 5) demonstrated restlessness or marked slowness; 6) daily fatigue; 7) daily feelings of worthlessness or excessive inappropriate guilt; 8) diminished ability to think or concentrate, or indecisiveness; 9) thoughts of death or suicide.[8]

To conclude this section, two points are noteworthy. First, different as they are, the dark night and depression are interconnected. Any serious believer experiences some aspects of the dark night, during short or prolonged periods; this is an opportunity to know oneself better psychologically by identifying one's weaknesses. It is also an opportunity to become more compassionate toward those who are suffering from their weaknesses.

Second, when a hitherto unknown type of trial takes place, we are taken by surprise and, since we are disoriented, we find it very hard. However, the second time it happens, it is less tough, because we have begun to learn how to react in an atmosphere of trust and even of gratitude for the opportunity to grow in faith, hope, love, and detachment, however agonizingly. It is also an opportunity to become more compassionate toward those who are suffering from their weaknesses and to learn how to love unconditionally.[9] Thus, moving out of a painful trial is a process involving a succession of small steps.[10]

---

8. Zagano and Gillespie, "Embracing Darkness," 58. The list of symptoms comes from *The Diagnostic and Statistical Manual of Mental Disorders*, 4th edition, published by the American Psychiatric Association.

9. This is what Henri Nouwen learned during his depression. See Nouwen, *Inner Voice*.

10. I thank Joseph Guido, OP, for helping me to improve the first draft of this section.

The Psychic, the Social, and the Spiritual

The development of the human being requires the interaction of three fundamental dimensions: the psychic, the social, and the spiritual. In the 1960s, a good number of psychologists who were writing about self-actualization paid little attention to the social context. Because of this lacuna, today their fine theories look rather removed from real life. Coming before the economic recession of the late 1970s, the atmosphere of that time was optimistic: everything seemed possible in the West. But the mood has changed. Statistics show that since the 1980s, even in rich countries the buying power of the majority of the population has slowly decreased, while the wealth of the 1 percent has increased year by year. This factor makes the superficial pursuit of self-actualization more difficult, as the price of apartments, hotels, restaurants, travel, vacation spots, and so on has been steadily mounting.

Even though the revenues of the middle class improved in the 1990s, psychological issues need to be related to other phenomena that affect collectivities. For the last two decades or so, some authors have placed the ideal of self-realization within its real social and economic setting.[11] Certain psychologists have insisted that problems within the home arise in large part from unhealthy tensions and dissatisfactions at work. The job itself may be insignificant or merely routine. Moreover, interpersonal relations at work are generally insipid, sometimes difficult, and seldom satisfying. Finally, it is not always evident to the workers how they are contributing to the general good of society.

On each of these points, a Christian vision of life, coupled with some psychological knowledge, can enable an individual to escape one's blindness with respect to social and financial situations. This tall order consists in forgoing apathy and fostering more initiative, patience, and hope. When one discovers in faith a reason for living as well as profound peace, and when one is capable of relating to others with serenity and humor, with self-respect and esteem for them, then one is able to recognize what one's commitments can

11. For example, Yankelovich, *New Rules*.

and cannot give, and one discerns what may be changed now and what may perhaps be changed later.

One area where many readjustments are needed consists in relationships between men and women. The numerous problems of which feminist writings inform us must be heard, reflected upon, and treated with tact. For a married couple, the division of work should not be immutable. Kindness, empathy, a critical mind, and a capacity for confrontation and negotiation must be present if people are going to make good decisions about such questions as the following: What friends and social contacts will we choose? How much contact will we have with our respective families? How many children will we have and when? What are our priorities for allocating our money? If both of us get promising job offers in different cities, which one shall we accept? If one of us wishes to pursue a degree, will the other be the sole support? In discussing these problems, the partners must be careful that the religious motivation of self-transcendence does not make them lose sight of the psychological dimension.

One must also make room for initiatives and creativity at home as well as in other settings. In democratic societies, there are many voluntary associations directed toward widely different objectives. Christians should encourage one another to recognize the significance of such commitments and to find those that suit them. Aside from its intrinsic value, a commitment to church or society that makes the best use of someone's talents can do much to balance family life and work.

A willingness to be involved with others will contribute much in the effort to achieve self-actualization in an evangelical perspective. Passivity is fatal. When people perceive that they have practically nothing to say either about the organization of their work or about society in general, their interest flows back into their private life. What they vaguely know and yet are reluctant to admit is that even their private life is largely regulated from outside. Alienation in regard to the environment thus ensues. Whether alone or in a group, these people isolate themselves in superficial pastimes or other experiences. Unfortunately, counselors and psychotherapists often do little to sensitize their clients to the social dimensions of their problems. Being too readily willing themselves to accept society's rules—which they mistake for "reality"—they do not help their clients go against the dominant disvalues. In the prevailing relativism, even true values are seen only as a means to individualistic self-realization. The slogan is "If pursuing that particular value makes you happy, go for it!"

Michael Lerner denounces the powerlessness that affects a large part of the American public in the face of deplorable conditions in their society.[12] He finds that the ideology of "meritocracy" blames individuals for their problems. Denying the economic, social, and political causes of these problems, this ideology makes people believe that it is up to individuals alone to fulfill themselves. Consequently, solutions to their difficulties are sought through improved health, sports, or attitude changes brought about in small groups. There is no recognition of the fact that frustration arises from the lack of change in the economy.

Lerner uses the term "surplus powerlessness" for the belief that ordinary people who are dissatisfied with society can do nothing to change it fundamentally. People have let themselves be convinced that human nature is essentially egotistical, self-interested, and eager to succeed at the expense of others. Not expecting any true solidarity from their fellow citizens, they conclude that they are bound to remain passive and let the financial and political elite control money, the mass media, and public opinion. They are convinced that, despite all their efforts, defeat is inevitable. When people are really sure that they do not deserve success, they resign themselves to be losers so that they can continue to blame and denigrate themselves and others.

Such is the prophetic analysis presented by Lerner. After the socio-political disappointments of the late 1960s, he gave up teaching philosophy in a university, obtained his doctorate in clinical psychology, and joined a group of psychiatrists, psychologists, social workers, family therapists, labor leaders, and activists to form an institute for reflection and psycho-social action. He is typical

12. Lerner, *Surplus Powerlessness*.

of a minority in wealthy countries, continuing to think freely and to discuss strategies that might promote interaction among the psychic, the social, and the spiritual.

Lerner preaches the renunciation of riches, security, and reputation gained at others' expense along with the rejection of the ideology of powerlessness. He urges a renewal of hope with the help of the great religious traditions of humankind. He suggests that authentic communities be created where people learn to listen, to dialogue, to respect one another, to accept imperfection, to understand common problems, and to be anxious that the group progress together as human beings. Finally, he welcomes initiatives toward collaboration with other groups and hopes that this kind of activity will, in time, generate a mass movement.

This chapter has emphasized rhythms, readjustments, as well as interactions between the psychic, the social, and the spiritual in the process of self-actualization. The above example illustrates the reemergence of values close to Gospel radicalism in a milieu where one would perhaps not expect to find them. This says much about the action of the Holy Spirit in our world.

Conclusion

In the course of this undertaking, a double conviction has propelled us: living faith is both inculturated and countercultural. Notice how the following two texts from St. Paul's letters balance each other.

> Whatever is true, whatever is honorable, whatever is just, whatever is pure, whatever is pleasing, whatever is commendable, if there is any excellence and if there is anything worthy of praise, think about these things. (Phil 4:8)

> Do not be conformed to this world, but be transformed by the renewing of your minds, so that you may discern what is the will of God—what is good and acceptable and perfect. (Rom 12:2)

The Gospel is transformative of culture, not by merely adapting itself to it, but through sifting, purifying, and strengthening the valuable components of that culture. In our contemporary world, one of the paramount values is self-actualization. Accordingly, we have tackled this issue: How can we be inculturated and countercultural *in a discerning manner*?

In this inquiry, we looked for a concept that would help us establish connections between the various aspects of the problem under discussion. The human openness to reality has been this operative linchpin. In analyzing defective forms of self-transcendence and of self-actualization, the first two chapters showed that those shortcomings derive from a lack of respect for the reality of the acting subject and for the reality of others. Chapter 3 drew attention to the intentionality in the depths of human nature, namely the capacity to be open to and interested in reality, especially interpersonal and social reality. Our desire to know and love raises questions and leads to acts that promote what is truly good. In chapter 4, we listened to radical texts of the New Testament that appeared as the exact opposites to any sort of self-assertion. Chapter 5 urged us to acknowledge a reality infinitely more vast and noble than any goal envisaged by ordinary human wisdom. This reality is called the kingdom of God—that is, what God wants to actualize among human beings.

Thanks to this opening up to reality, chapter 6 established that despite the fact that self-actualization and the radical Gospel clash with one another in a great number of instances, a synthesis is not only desirable but also possible in the lives of people who respond to divine grace. However, this synthesis cannot take place purely on the basis of the human tendency toward self-actualization. Instead, it is the Christian vision of life that must integrate the tendency toward self-actualization into a larger drama. The process of integration requires that the drive toward self-realization be deep and critical enough to recognize its own deviations while accentuating its strengths and welcoming meaning and values that shift it into a richer context. In chapter 7, we illustrated various difficulties to be taken into account in the journey toward a fuller and more satisfying unification.

The decisive attitude consists in gratefully receiving a definite plenitude from our loving Creator, either through human mediation or in prayerful immediacy. We experience deep joy provided we accept the fact that our self-actualization remains partial. We can then take in stride the inevitable alternation of ups and downs, of progress and crisis, of temporary stagnations followed by fresh starts. Throughout the unique itinerary that constitutes our life, it is up to each of us to find our own forms of Gospel radicalism as we are attentive to the needs of others, to our personal gifts, and to the voice of the Holy Spirit.

Bibliography

Aquinas, Thomas. *Commentary on Aristotle's Nicomachean Ethics.* Translated by C. I. Litzinger. Notre Dame, IN: Dumb Ox, 1993.
———. *Summa contra Gentiles.* Translated by Vernon J. Bourke. Notre Dame, IN: University of Notre Dame Press, 1975.
———. *Summa Theologiae.* Translated by Fathers of the English Dominican Province. 3rd ed. 22 vols. Vol. 1. London: Burns, Oates and Washbourne, 1916.
Aristotle. *Nicomachean Ethics.* Translated by Terence Irwin. 2nd ed. Indianapolis: Hackett, 1999.
Augustine. *Responses to Miscellaneous Questions.* Translated by Boniface Ramsey. Hyde Park, NY: New City, 2008.
———. *Teaching Christianity.* Translated by Edmund Hill. Hyde Park, NY: New City, 1996.
Barron, Robert. *Renewing Our Hope: Essays for the New Evangelization.* Washington, DC: Catholic University of America Press, 2020.
Barthes, Roland. *The Pleasure of the Text.* Translated by Richard Miller. New York: Hill and Wang, 1975.
Barzun, Jacques. *From Dawn to Decadence: 500 Years of Western Cultural Life, 1500 to the Present.* New York: Perennial, 2000.
Bellah, Robert N., et al. *Habits of the Heart: Individualism and Commitments in American Life.* New York: Harper and Row, 1985.
Bergson, Henri. *Mind-Energy: Lectures and Essays.* Westport, CT: Greenwood, 1975.
Bonhoeffer, Dietrich. *The Cost of Discipleship.* 6th ed. London: SCM, 1959.
Brown, Brené. *Daring Greatly: How the Courage to Be Vulnerable Transforms the Way We Live, Love, Parent, and Lead.* New York: Gotham, 2012.
Burton, Tara Isabella. *Strange Rites: New Religions for a Godless World.* New York: Public Affairs, 2020.
Butler, Joseph. *Five Sermons Preached at the Rolls Chapel.* Indianapolis: Hackett, 1983.
Calvin, John. *Institutes of the Christian Religion.* Translated by Henry Beveridge. Grand Rapids: Eerdmans, 1989.

BIBLIOGRAPHY

Caruso, Igor A. *Psychanalyse et synthèse personnelle*. Paris: Desclée de Brouwer, 1959.
Conn, Walter E. *Conscience: Development and Self-Transcendence*. Birmingham, AL: Religious Education, 1981.
———. *The Desiring Self: Rooting Pastoral Counseling and Spiritual Direction in Self-Transcendence*. Mahwah, NJ: Paulist, 1998.
Connolly, Cyril. *Journal and Memoir*. Edited by David Pryce-Jones. London: Collins, 1983.
de Chardin, Teilhard. *The Phenomenon of Man*. Translated by Bernard Wall. New York: Harper & Row, 1965.
de Saint-Exupéry, Antoine. *The Little Prince*. Translated by Katherine Woods. New York: Harcourt, Brace, 1943.
de Sales, Francis. *The Love of God: A Treatise*. Translated by Vincent Kerns. Westminster, MD: Newman, 1962.
Doran, Robert M. *Psychic Conversion and Theological Foundations: Toward a Reorientation of the Human Sciences*. Chico, CA: Scholars, 1981.
Dupont, Jacques. *Les béatitudes*. 2nd ed. 3 vols. Paris: Gabalda, 1958–1973.
Eliot, George. *Wise, Witty and Tender Sayings in Prose and Verse*. Edited by Alexander Main. Edinburgh: William Blackwood, 1873.
Fackenheim, Emil L. *Quest for Past and Future: Essays in Jewish Theology*. Boston: Beacon, 1970.
FitzGerald, Constance. "Impasse and Dark Night." In *Women's Spirituality: Resources for Christian Development*, edited by Joann Wolski Conn. New York: Paulist, 1996.
Francis. *Fratelli Tutti*. Vatican City: Libreria Editrice Vatican, 2020. https://www.vatican.va/content/francesco/en/encyclicals/documents/papa-francesco_20201003_enciclica-fratelli-tutti.html.
Frankl, Viktor E. *Psychotherapy and Existentialism: Selected Papers on Logotherapy*. New York: Simon and Schuster, 1967.
———. *The Will to Meaning: Foundations and Applications of Logotherapy*. New York: New American Library, 1969.
Freud, Sigmund. *Civilization and Its Discontents*. Translated by James Strachey. New York: Norton.
Fromm, Erich. *The Art of Loving*. New York: Harper and Row, 1956.
———. *Man for Himself: An Inquiry into the Psychology of Ethics*. New York: Rinehart, 1947.
Gourgues, Michel. *Jésus devant sa passion et sa mort*. Paris: Cerf, 1979.
Hobbes, Thomas. *Leviathan*. Edited by Edwin Curly. Indianapolis, IN: Hackett, 1994.
Hunter, Graeme. *Pascal the Philosopher: An Introduction*. Toronto: University of Toronto Press, 2013.
John of the Cross. *The Collected Works of St. John of the Cross*. Translated by Kieran Kavanaugh and Otilio Rodriguez. Rev. ed. Washington, D.C.: ICS, 1991.

Jullien, François. *Resources of Christianity*. Translated by Pedro Rodriguez. Cambridge, UK: Polity, 2021.
Kant, Immanuel. *Grounding for the Metaphysics of Morals*. Translated by James W. Ellington. Indianapolis: Hackett, 1993.
Kirkpatrick, Lee E. *Attachment, Evolution, and the Psychology of Religion*. New York: Guilford, 2005.
Klein, Melanie. *Envy and Gratitude*. New York: Basic, 1957.
Kristeva, Julia. *Black Sun: Depression and Melancholia*. Translated by Leon S. Roudiez. New York: Columbia University Press, 1989.
Lasch, Christopher. *The Minimal Self: Psychic Survival in Troubled Times*. New York: Norton, 1984.
Lerner, Michael. *Surplus Powerlessness: The Psychodynamics of Everyday Life and the Psychology of Individual and Social Transformation*. Atlantic Highlands, NJ: Humanities, 1991.
Lewis, C. S. *The Four Loves*. New York: Harcourt, Brace, 1960.
Locke, John. *The Second Treatise on Civil Government*. New York: Prometheus, 1986.
Lonergan, Bernard. *Method in Theology*. Collected Works of Bernard Lonergan. Edited by Robert M. Doran and John D. Dadosky. Vol. 14. Toronto: University of Toronto Press, 2017.
Lonergan, Bernard J. F. *Insight: A Study of Human Understanding*. Collected Works of Bernard Lonergan. Edited by Frederick E. Crowe and Robert M. Doran. Vol. 3. Toronto: University of Toronto Press, 1992.
Luther, Martin. *Christian Liberty*. Edited by Harold J. Grimm. Philadelphia: Fortress, 1985.
Main, John. *Moment of Christ: The Path of Meditation*. New York: Crossroad, 1984.
Manning, Patrick R. *Converting the Imagination: Teaching to Recover Jesus' Vision for Fullness of Life*. Eugene, OR: Pickwick, 2020.
Marcel, Gabriel. *Homo Viator: Introduction to a Metaphysic of Hope*. Translated by Emma Craufurd. London: Victor Gollancz, 1951.
———. *The Mystery of Being*. Vol. 2. Faith and Reality, Chicago: Regnery, 1960.
Marion, Jean-Luc. "The Reason of the Gift." In *Giveness and God: Questions of Jean-Luc Marion*, edited by Ian Leask and Eoin Cassidy, 101–34. New York: Fordham University Press, 2005.
Maslow, Abraham H. *Toward a Psychology of Being*. 3rd ed. New York: Wiley, 1968.
Matura, Thaddée. *Le radicalisme évangélique*. Paris: Cerf, 1978.
———. *Suivre Jésus*. Paris: Cerf, 1983.
May, Gerald G. *Care of Mind / Care of Spirit*. San Francisco: Harper & Row, 1982.
———. *The Dark Night of the Soul: A Psychiatrist Explores the Connection Between Darkness and Spiritual Growth*. San Francisco: HarperCollins, 2004.

BIBLIOGRAPHY

McCullough, David. *You Are Not Special ... and Other Encouragements*. New York: HarperCollins, 2014.

Moskowitz, Eva. *In Therapy We Trust: America's Obsession with Self-Fulfillment*. Baltimore: Johns Hopkins University Press, 2008.

Nietzche, Friedrich. *The Gay Science*. Edited by Bernard Williams. Translated by Josefine Nauckhoff. Cambridge, UK: Cambridge University Press, 2001.

Nouwen, Henri. *The Inner Voice of Love: A Journey through Anguish to Freedom*. New York: Image Books, 1998.

Novak, Philip. "Attention." In *Encyclopedia of Religion*, vol. 1, edited by Mircea Eliade, 501–509. New York: Macmillan, 1987.

Outka, Gene. *Agape: An Ethical Analysis*. New Haven, CT: Yale University Press, 1972.

Pascal, Blaise. *Oeuvres complètes*. Paris: Hachette, 1871. https://upload.wikimedia.org/wikipedia/commons/thumb/6/62/%C5%92uvres_compl%C3%A8tes_de_Blaise_Pascal_Hachette_1871%2C_vol2.djvu/page58-4267px-%C5%92uvres_compl%C3%A8tes_de_Blaise_Pascal_Hachette_1871%2C_vol2.djvu.jpg.

Piaget, Jean. *The Construction of Reality in the Child*. New York: Basic, 1954.

Pohier, Jacques. *God—In Fragments*. Translated by John S. Bowden. New York: Crossroad, 1986.

Reich, Wilhelm. *Character Analysis*. Translated by Vincent R. Carfagno. New York: Farrar, Straus and Giroux, 1972.

Ricoeur, Paul. *Oneself as Another*. Translated by Kathleen Blamey. Chicago: University of Chicago Press, 1992.

Rolheiser, Ronald. *Sacred Fire: A Vision for a Deeper Human and Christian Maturity*. New York: Random House, 2014.

Rousseau, Jean-Jacques. *The Creed of a Priest of Savoy*. Translated by Arthur H. Beattie. 2nd ed. New York: Continuum, 1988.

———. *A Discourse on Inequality*. Translated by Maurice Cranston. London: Penguin, 1984.

———. *Emile or On Education*. Translated by Allan Bloom. New York: Basic, 1979.

———. *Reveries of a Solitary Walker*. Translated by Russell Goulbourne. New York: Oxford University Press, 2011.

Roy, Louis. *Embracing Desire*. Translated by Robert Czerny, assisted by Pierrot Lambert. Eugene, OR: Wipf and Stock, 2019.

———. *Engaging the Thought of Bernard Lonergan*. Montreal: McGill-Queen's University Press, 2016.

———. *The Feeling of Transcendence, an Experience of God?* Translated by Pierre LaViolette and Anne Louise Mahoney. Eugene, OR: Wipf and Stock, 2020.

———. *God: Polarities in Language*. Forthcoming.

———. "Human Desire and Easter Faith." In *Jesus Crucified and Risen: Essays in Spirituality and Theology in Honor of Dom Sebastian Moore*, edited by

William P. Loewe and Vernon J. Gregson. Collegeville, MN: Liturgical Press, 1998.

———. *Mystical Consciousness: Western Perspectives and Dialogue with Japanese Thinkers*. Albany, NY: SUNY Press, 2003.

———. *The Three Dynamisms of Faith: Searching for Meaning, Fulfillment and Truth*. Washington, D.C.: Catholic University of America Press, 2017.

———. *Transcendent Experiences: Phenomenology and Critique*. Toronto: University of Toronto Press, 2001.

Selye, Hans. *Stress without Distress*. Philadelphia: Lippincott, 1974.

Sophocles. *Antigone*. Edited by Moses Hadas. Translated by Sir Richard Claverhouse Jebb. New York: Bantam, 1982.

Sorokin, Pitirim A. *The Reconstruction of Humanity*. Boston: Beacon Press, 1948.

Thielicke, Helmut. *Life Can Begin Again: Sermons on the Sermon on the Mount*. Translated by John W. Doberstein. Philadelphia: Fortress, 1963.

Trethowan, Illtyd. *Absolute Value: A Study in Christian Theism*. New York: Humanities, 1970.

Trilling, Lionel. *Sincerity and Authenticity*. Cambridge, MA: Harvard University Press, 1972.

Turkle, Sherry. *The Empathy Diaries: A Memoir*. New York: Penguin, 2021.

Vacek, Edward Collins. *Love, Human and Divine: The Heart of Christian Ethics*. Washington, D.C.: Georgetown University Press, 1994.

Weber, Max. *Politics as a Vocation*. Translated by H. H. Gerth and C. Wright Mills. Philadelphia: Fortress, 1965.

Weil, Simone. *Gravity and Grace*. Translated by Arthur Wills. New York: Putnam's Sons, 1952.

Wilkins, Jeremy. *Before Truth: Lonergan, Aquinas, and the Problem of Wisdom*. Washington, D.C.: Catholic University of America Press, 2018.

Williams, Rowan. *Luminaries: Twenty Lives that Illuminate the Christian Way*. London: SPCK, 2019.

Yankelovich, Daniel. *New Rules: Searching for Self-Fulfillment in a World Turned Upside Down*. New York: Random House, 1981.

Zagano, Phyllis, and C. Kevin Gillespie. "Embracing Darkness: A Theological and Psychological Case Study of Mother Teresa." *Spiritus* 1, no. 10 (2010): 52–75.

www.ingramcontent.com/pod-product-compliance
Lightning Source LLC
Chambersburg PA
CBHW030903170426
43193CB00009BA/725